When India Dismissed It's Naval Chief

The Admiral Vishnu Bhagwat episode

Cmde Ranjit Rai (Retd.)

Brigadier R.P. Singh (Retd.)

ISBN 13: 9789385699054 ISBN 10: 93-85699-05-9

Published by

Frontier India Technology

No 22, 4th Floor, MK Joshi Building, Devi Chowk, Shastri
Nagar,
Dombivli West, Maharashtra, India. 421202
http://frontierindia.org

DEDICATION

To the Indian Navy

CONTENTS

INTRODUCTION

In the turbulent times of post POKHRAN 'Shakti' nuclear tests cum IRBM AGNI II, India faced some flak and a difficult attitude from the West, whilst internally it is embroiled with coalition and backbiting politics. At such a time there could be no more interesting, yet challenging security related subject to write a book devoted to it, than the dismissal of Admiral Vishnu Bhagwat on 30 December 1998 from his post as the Chief of Naval Staff. I got to know Vishnu in 1955, when we both joined the NDA as term-mates of the 14th course and have served together in the same training ships and in the Fleet and Naval Headquarters. So I am encouraged to offer a view on what will be part of India's military history, and to offer some lessons learnt from that unfortunate episode. In 1997, Admiral Mansoor Al Haq, CNS of the Pakistan Navy, was made to resign in Pakistan on allegations of corruption and another Naval Chief resigned in Sri Lanka, but my search showed that almost no serving Naval Chief has been sacked in the world, in the manner Vishnu was dismissed. The action was unprecedented, and to fell a serviceman's pride without adequate evidence is anathema in military circles. The sacking became controversial and one wonders if there was no other honourable way out.

Four years prior to this, Admiral Jeremy Michael Boorda, the CNO of the US Navy, the only officer who had risen from the lowest rank as an enlisted man to become Chief of the US Navy, was found to be wearing a Vietnam battle zone clasp on his ribbon in his decorations, which he had not earned, and the media blew it up. One afternoon he left his office for lunch and shot himself in his Admiral's quarters. Admiral Frank Benton Kelso II of "attack on Libya fame", another CNO, was found guilty of covering up allegations of the Tailhook Conference (aviators get together) where women were molested and he was reprimanded and allowed to serve his remaining months. General Douglas MacArthur was chosen to lead US Forces in the Korean War in 1950 and President Harry S. Truman removed him from Command in 1951 when he refused to limit the scope of the war. It was an operational decision he refused to obey. Therefore, it makes for interesting research on the backdrop, the sacking, the reasons attributed for it and the legal aspects of the case, and why Bhagwat was not court-martialed if he had transgressed Naval Discipline or breached National Security.

In the Indian Navy's brief history Admirals R.H. Tahiliani, Ex CNS, Vice Admiral S.C. Chopra, Ex VCNS, R.P. Sawhney, Ex DCNS have all faced courts martial for hazarding their ships INS Vikrant, Betwa and Kirpan as Captains. All three were honourably acquitted and rose to high ranks. I, too, faced a court-martial for hazarding INS Vindhyagiri as the Captain when an errant merchantman 'Sebastiano' collided with my ship in a squall in1984. I was honourably acquitted. Thanks to that event, my knowledge of Naval Regulations was enhanced by a fine officer, Late Commodore Arvind Dabir, who defended me. There are a lot of loopholes in Naval Law and in my case in 1984, the CNS (NHQ) desired to courts martial me but my Flag Officer In Chief Commanding Western Naval Command Vice Admiral S. Mookerjee did not agree. The Regulations, Indian Navy had to be amended and this took five months for the CNS to get the powers which earlier rules did not permit. I am therefore sure this particular case of Bhagwat lends itself to inquiry to ensure there are clarifications and changes to the Regulations and the Constitution, as Military Law in a democracy is an evolving process and we have a long way to go to bring the three services under a common law. In India, the status of the President as the Supreme Commander of the Armed forces also needs defining for he does sign the file of appointment of the CNS, but need not for the dismissal. The subject is dealt with in this book.

Vishnu, on the afternoon of 30th December, had concluded a call to Rear Admiral Raja Menon to congratulate him on the lecture, which he had attended that morning as Chairman Chiefs of Staff Committee. Menon had been given a grant to prepare a paper on 'Nuclear Theology for India' and the lecture was a preview of his thesis presented at the USI. Mr. K. Subramanyan and many nuclear experts were also present and the question and answer session was extremely lively, as the nuclear template of India is still under debate and articulation. Times of India of that day and in earlier editions had carried bold editorials in support of Vishnu Bhagwat's nonacceptance of Vice Admiral Harinder Singh as the Deputy Chief of Naval Staff (DCNS), which had been approved by the Appointments Committee of the Cabinet. The cadence and writing gave hints of Mr. K. Subramanyam's fluent pen and when I questioned him that morning in the vicinity of Bhagwat in the USI foyer, he neither confirmed nor denied it, and asserted editorials were anonymous. This subject of discord between the Cabinet and the Navy Chief on Harinder, whom I knew as a professional and capable shipmate, had been alive and on the forefront in the media and so many eyes were trained on Admiral Vishnu Bhagwat. He appeared unaware that Sushil Kumar was airborne on his way to New Delhi, as he tasked USI to widely circulate the video of the lecture and asked Menon to give a similar presentation to the Chiefs of Staff Committee. He added that knowledge of nuclear issues is lacking among the politicians and they may like to be educated.

The book in discussion also covers some aspects of India's security and management of higher defence. After the sacking, not only has the Indian public been made privy to security matters and some intrigues of defence purchases, but they have also witnessed the Prime Minister Shri Atal Behari Vajpayee, the Defence Minister Shri George Fernandes, his party secretary Shrimati Jaya Jaitley and the Defence Spokesmen and many others go public in the print and TV media with accusations against the dismissed Admiral. He has not been offered an official platform to defend himself. He has had to resort to the media and table a sworn affidavit. He has been severally accused of breach of national security, defiance of

Cabinet orders, tampering with Annual Confidential Reports, false statements and other wild allegations while legal experts have questioned the very validity of the act of dismissal itself. The manner in which Vishnu Bhagwat was unseated from his corner white office in Room 190 of South Block connotes all the trapping of a high voltage drama, resembling a coup. The Ministry of Defence issued a hurriedly edited 124-page booklet in defence of the Ministry's actions and some parts of that which include earlier classified material is also included in this book.

The RM's actions seem to have been taken with trepidation that his coup may misfire, and he was taking no chances. The nation heard of this drama in the late evening news and many senior officers serving and retired, were not so upset at the sacking, as the manner of the sacking. It had no signs of civility, but as a doctor in this case Fernandes would say if surgery is the answer, then so be it. In hindsight, that seems to have been Fernandes' aim. The issue needs historical recording and debate, hence this book. Commodore P.K. Jain (Retd) who has served as a Staff Officer to CNS Admiral Jal Cursetji assisted me in this endeavour.

I have tried to draw fairly and selectively from the media and from my own personal knowledge of the fine Indian Navy and as a contemporary of Bhagwat. I have also made inquiries and perused writs and affidavits filed on oath. Without doubt, the ignominious removal has more than stirred up a hornet's nest. It has let the political parties give vent to their machinations tarnishing in the bargain the image of the Indian Navy with fecal matter. Issues that are not relevant were magnified and vendetta seekers and media savvy journalists had a field day. The Bhagwat episode became a tool in the hands of the political parties. The available facts of the case are therefore put down in this book as a duty to the nation and for posterity as one record and view of events of the times. This is done without fear or favour so that present and future generations are made aware of the conspiracies, legal battles and mudslinging that went on, between the years 1988 to 2000 in La Affaire Vishnu Bhagwat. Bhagwat with full pension and now rank stands re-instated in 2012. I have no doubt that the Indian Navy it is in capable hands today, that there should be no problems which it will not be able to overcome and live up to its motto.

I address this book to every inquisitive man, woman and teenager in India. If on one hand I have exposed matters by oversimplification, I beg their indulgence in National interest but national security is the subject. Service leaders have to lead their men to death in war and peace and service before self, is still the credo.

Brigadier R.P. Singh who retired as the Deputy Judge Advocate of the Indian Army has a sharp legal brain, deep knowledge of Military and Civil Law. He readily agreed to co-author this book and add to the legal aspects of the Bhagwat case. These chapters should be of interest to lawyers and others to clear the cobwebs raised in the media, and a fervent hope that the three services will bring together their legal systems for better coordination and to keep up with the times and abide by the Constitution. The framers of the Indian Constitution did not have any one with a military background and maybe some clauses need to be added. For well it was scribed "Justice is not a cloistered virtue; she must be allowed to suffer the scrutiny and respectful though outspoken comments of the ordinary man " - Extract from a Judgement by Lord Atkin, 1936.

Finally, the manner of appointment and then the sacking of Admiral Vishnu Bhagwat could have been better handled if India's higher management of Defence had a Single head like a Chief of Defence Staff to take on responsibility and also be the senior advisor to the Defence Minister, which task has been handled ineptly by Defence Secretaries who are eminently unqualified for the task. This also, has led to "bureaucrat vs. the services" unease and needs redressing. A reorganisation of India's Defence structure has been promised by the Defence Minister.

This book was published as SACKED OR SUNK: Admiral Vishnu Bhagwat.

POTRAIT OF EX-ADMIRAL VISHNU BHAGWAT, PVSM AVSM - A THUMB NAIL SKETCH

Vishnu, the name is derived and adopted in India from one of the triumvirate of the Hindu pantheon. Brahma is considered the creator, Vishnu the preserver and Shiva is the destroyer. These are the Gods that form the bedrock of a Hindu's belief and the many other gods are reincarnations of these three. Whether Vishnu in his service career lived up to that epithet, is up to the readers to judge, but no one can deny he has had one of the most impressive track and career records in the Indian Navy. Most of his appointments were weighty and he had passed the rigorous sieve of the selection process of the Indian Navy. As his term-mate, who competed with him, I can state he had the quality of tenacity and perseverance in plenty. In my meager research of him, this also came out in abundance and the manner in which he doggedly opposed George Fernandes and Ajit Kumar whilst in office and after being sacked speak for themselves. Great, famous and controversial personalities are always delightful subjects for biographies and this thumbnail sketch of Vishnu Bhagwat is a rung in this book of my analysis of the historic event that brought down a government in 1999.

Misra Vishnu Kumar Sharma, as he was known when he joined NDA and I met him first, was born in Jullundar on 8, October 1939, and is the son of Bhagwat Prasad Sharma and Kamla. His father was Lieutenant Colonel Sharma of the Indian Army, and Bhagwat had a brother in the first course of the JSW. Bhagwat was educated at the prestigious Lawrence School, Sanawar near Simla, from where he completed his Senior Cambridge in 1954. He was lean, tall and tenacious and began to show qualities of achievement at school. He was awarded the Public School Scholarship Award by the Government of India, Ministry of Education from 1951 to 1954. He appeared for the NDA open UPSC examination for the 14th JSW/NDA course and Misra Vishnu Kumar Sharma successfully qualified and joined the NDA with the other 286 cadets in July 1955 as a Naval cadet. That is the first time we met. In all fairness it must be admitted that there were only some 36 Naval cadets in that batch and to get Navy as one's choice was to be in the upper reaches of the merit list. Bhagwat reported to the Able Squadron and as we all got down to the rough and tumble of training, our days were spent in parade physical and equestrian training along with academics and service subjects like map-reading, military history and the like. Later, he was transferred to Charlie Squadron. Vishnu did show the streak of a loner, thinker and a tenacious plodder who did not excel in sports and academics. The 14th course was indeed one of the largest courses to join the NDA and was the second to be inducted at the new site at Pune. It was Pandit Nehru's dream and desire came true when he said, "there should be only one academy to train for the three services" as early as 22 September 1945 on file. In the NDA, stress was laid on development of character, self-reliance, leadership and self-discipline; and led by Major General Habibullah, the team of officers, civilian instructors and JCO's including the British Regiment's Sergeant Major Ayling who supervised drill practice. They were a dedicated and able lot. The NDA is set in a valley adjoining the Lake Khadakvasla and is an ideal site for basic military and nautical training and is close to Sinhgad Fort. Folktale goes that the valley used to resound with cries of 'Khadakvasla' or the abode of the 'Sword' as the village across the lake was called. It provided poetic justification to the establishment of a training academy in the valleys and dales, the very hunting grounds of Shivaji and his valiant men. There is no denying that the period of our training in NDA, July 1955-December 1958 were molding years and streaks of over-zealousness and patriotism were evident in the character of Vishnu. Later, they were to develop into signs of leftish leanings and markedly pro-Soviet and anti-west.

The 14th course was indeed an above average course at NDA besides being the largest. It produced more blues in sports than any other and in academics, drama and cultural activities. The Commandant who was a dedicated soul made us climb heights. Even as first termers, the 14th course took part in a parade for Lord Mountbatten and the event received accolades. As time went on, the 14th course produced two Chiefs of staff – Vishnu and Ved Malik, innumerable Marshals, Generals, Vice-Admiral P.S. Das and Air Vice Marshals Singh and Kamlesh Khanna. No course so far has exceeded the total number and the course holds decorations. Berry got the MVC and Roy and Choudhary the VrC.

It is therefore, with some pride, one writes that Vishnu was the product of an excellent and above-average course, which today has a strong association. However, for some reasons, he never joined the course functions. After passing out of NDA, we all joined INS, Tir in July 1958 after taking passage to Trincomalee in INS Krishna and took part in joint exercises with the Royal, Pakistan, Australian and New Zealand Navies. The ship made calls at Singapore, Saigon, Brunei and some other ports and Late Commodore (then Commander) Dolly Mehta was our Commanding Officer and Late Admiral V.P.S. Shekawat (then known as V.P. Singh) was our training officer. Vishnu did not care much for jaunts ashore and slogged on board. He worked tenaciously hard and even though I came first in order of merit and got my branch changed from engineering to executive, Vishnu i.e. Misra Vishnu Kumar Sharma was awarded the Coveted Telescope as the best all-round cadet on INS, Tir in 1958. Once again on board INS Mysore, our term-mate midshipman P.S. Das, a brilliant officer who rose to Vice-Admiral secured a first class in Midshipman's board, but Vishnu was awarded the best all-round Midshipman's Sword of Honour. We were all commissioned on 1st January 1960. In the courses that followed P.S. Das gained a record 12 out of 12 months seniority, I came next, Ravi Sharma third and Vishnu Bhagwat was fourth. That seniority continued till P.S. Das in 1964 as a young Lieutenant lost 6 months and I moved to the top of the 14th course list.

Vishnu went on to carve an enviable and impeccable track record of appointments in his progression in the Navy. He served in INS Tir during the 1961 Goa Operation, was an instructor in NDA which is prestigious and in 1965 we were selected to attend specialization courses. P.S. Das and Vishnu Bhagwat got Communications and I got Navigation and Direction. I recall Vishnu working late into the nights at Cochin and was nicknamed the plodder. Later in life, in a letter to Vishnu, his Commanding-in-chief had this to say, "you are a workaholic in the finest sense of the word."

As a Senior Lieutenant, Bhagwat's appointments were all high profile. He was Squadron Communications Officer on INS Rajput and then Flag Lieutenant to Admiral A.K. Chaterjee. He accompanied the Admiral to Australia, New Zealand and Thailand in 1969. On promotion to Lieutenant Commander, Bhagwat went early to the Defence Services Staff College in 1971 and was graded Directing Staff. In December, Bhagwat joined INS Tir as Executive Officer and participated in the 4, December 1971 attack on Karachi. The towing ship INS Tir towed the missile boats some distance from Karachi and let them loose and he took much credit for it in later years as one of the few officers of his seniority with war record. Thereafter, on promotion to Commander, Bhagwat was the Deputy Director of Personnel under Vice-Admiral R.K.S. Ghanohi and got command of INS Amini a Petya and followed up to be a Fleet Operation Officer of the Western Fleet. These are very challenging assignments, having myself been a Deputy Director in NHQ, commanded a Petya INS Kavaralti and been a Fleet Operations

Officer for two years. Surely, till date, Bhagwat was doing very well.

As Captain, and the n Commander, Bhagwat was in NHQ as Joint Director Naval Training and then briefly DNT, but his involvement in the Perspective Planning Group under the then Vice-Chief Vice-Admiral R.H. Tahiliani gave him insights into the template Tahiliani was formulating for the Navy and chalking the career prospects of each and every officer of the rank of Captain and above. The Navy has been through a Cadre Review. From there it was onto pre-Command training at Pote in Russia in 1981 to become Commanding Officer of INS Ranjit in USSR. A controversy erupted between him and his superior, the Naval Attache Commodore, later Rear Admiral Ravi, who did not give him a good report. This, it is rumored, was later amended by the Ambassador and has come up in correspondence. On board INS Ranjit, a midshipman shot his colleague dead and Bhagwat came out with a mild reprimand, whilst his Executive Officer work the rap. Command of INS Ranjit was prestigious and a proud Bhagwat received the well-deserved AVSM in 1986 as a Captain for setting high operational standards. Thereafter, it was a course at National Defence College in 1986 and the coveted post of Naval Assistant to the Chief of Naval Staff R.H. Tahiliani events and to Rear Admiral, Vice-Admiral and Chief of Naval Staff are threaded separately. In all fairness one must pen that few have been able to chalk up such professional appointments.

Vishnu was one who lived a spartan life, never smoked or drank and did not take well those who indulged in these two habits, and could never understand why they did so. He was a stickler for discipline, and ambitious in a good sense. He married Niloufer, a fiery lawyer he met in Pune, and has two fine children. When I first wrote this book, his daughter Roshni was a doctor undergoing specialization in Pediatrics, and son Jawahar is a Lieutenant in the Navy undergoing training for submarine branch. Mrs. Bhagwat worked hard from her small office in Flora Fountain, supported many causes and visited USSR more than once and genuinely believed that her husband was done wrong. She was Vishnu's wife and lawyer, an unusual combination.

GEORGE FERNANDES' 90-MINUTE TELEVISION INTERVIEW ON DOORDARSHAN AND 100 - PAGE BOOKLET - AN ANALYSIS

Shri George Fernandes went public on national television in April 1999 and bared secret naval matters in an interview to defend his controversy-ridden action of 30th December when he sacked Admiral Vishnu Bhagwat. Karan Thapar, the interviewer, cleverly baited Fernandes on charges already orchestrated in the media against him, and asked leading questions to reveal Bhagwat's supposed malafide and anti-national actions. Thapar extracted confirmations and denials, as one would in a good cross-examination by a criminal defence lawyer, who has prepared his case well for his client, Fernandes. Retired term mates and colleagues of Bhagwat like me who served as Captains of Western Fleet ships at the same time as Bhagwat and thereafter in NHQ between 1985-1990, were unaware of all details of the plots and legal exchanges, which had plagued the Indian Navy during the period 1989-91. The interview was an eye opener as matters were revealed from the proverbial horse's mouth. Fernandes vividly recalled events, names, promotion board proceedings and read directly from highly confidential files.

Doordarshan left no stops and used its latest equipment and transmitters to give viewers a clear picture. At the end of the viewing of the two-part long serial, it reminded of one Charles Ruff's arguments delivered from a wheelchair in defence of President Bill Clinton in the Senate Impeachment trial. Ruff unequivocally extolled to the learned Chief Justice Warren and the 100 Senators of the United States, that the No.1 crime of high demeanor envisaged by the founding fathers for impeachment was that of "vacating records." It is the same charge leveled by an emotionally charged Fernandes against Bhagwat. Treason came next, according to Ruff, and the nuclear submarine revelations came near it, according to Fernandes. Corruption ranked third. In USA Ruff confidently argued Clinton was guilty of none of these wrong doings but got involved with a young dark-haired intelligent and sexy intern Monica Lewinsky. It is now clear she was flaunting her sex appeal in the White House, to which the President with a track record full of many dalliances, succumbed. In USA the issue rocked the nation and has now passed over after an open trial. In India there is need for a full blue ribbon inquiry and this meagre book is to provoke thought on the subject.

The naval rules permit the Chiefs of Naval Staff to overwrite and mark up or down arbitrarily any report of any officer of the rank of Commander, Acting Captain and above even if they never set eyes on him or observed the performance of that officer. This is not so in the large Indian Army or the Air Force to such a large degree. This is the relic of a small Navy and because the next selective rank after Captain is that of a Rear Admiral. Commodore in the

IN is times scale rank. This was a privilege accorded to the Chief of a small Navy, which was run like a club till the 70s, but has grown big, and its personnel matters have suffered on account of this. Fernandes has revealed some snippets of misuse of the powers when he talked of Commander Bandhopadhya's reports as Assistant Naval Attache in Moscow, when Bhagwat wanted him recalled. Thapar and the media have mistakenly upgraded him to Commodore rank. Fernandes stated that Bhagwat had over-written reports and ruined careers. In the media, Commodores B.K. Ray's and Rusi Contractor's reports were reported, which possibly made differences to their careers. The College of Defence Management, Secunderabad, was tasked to do a study of the anomalies in naval reporting system and other lacunae in the 80s, but like many other reports, including the Arun Singh report, it collects dust in the serpentine rooms of South Block's labyrinth.

After four months commencing 30 Dec 98, the day when the Chief of Naval Staff Admiral Vishnu Bhagwat lost the pleasure of the President under Article 310 of the Constitution and was relieved of his post for unfitness to carry out his duties, the nation witnessed a slanging match on who was right and who was wronged. A political storm erupted and no day passed in the ensuing few months without comments, statements, allegations and counter allegations in the media. Personal and confidential reports of naval officers appeared in the print media and discussed brazenly on television. A retired submariner, Commodore V.K. Choudhry, who works in Moscow, was given a clean chit by the Rakshya Mantri of not dealing in arms and it has raised eyebrows. If the Defence Minister is to be believed, it appears Bhagwat as Chief of Naval Staff of the Indian Navy and even some of his predecessors are guilty of vacating records. Bhagwat, in his 400-plus page writ petition No. 2757 filed in the High Court of Bombay in 1990 by his wife and lawyer Mrs. Nilofeur Bhagwat described separately, had squarely put the then Chief of Naval Staff Admiral J.G. Nadkarni and the next senior most Vice Admiral S. Jain in the dock by accusing them of vacating his records. Both officers filed affidavits but their explanations were considered legally far from clear and doubts lingered.

Fernandes read out some reports tendered by Nadkarni on the Bhagwat's writ, which are revealing of the times. Nadkarni desired but could not Court-Martial or dismiss Bhagwat. What was then common knowledge was the Navy experienced an internecine battle for the top slot for Nadkarni's successor. Camps got formed and plagued the Navy's equilibrium, thanks to Bhagwat's allegations against one and sundry in the writ. In the tussle for the top slot many including the media and especially the Blitz and Business Standard claimed that Vice Admiral S. Jain lost out to Admiral L. Ramdas for the top slot as CNS because a nexus existed between then Rear Admiral Bhagwat, his writ petition and Vice Admiral Ramdas's ambitions. This was dismissed as speculation by many of us on the scene at that time who tried to pin the truth without success. Now many coincidences have emerged and Bhagwat was favoured when Ramdas was CNS.

When Ramdas became Chief in 1990, he set a new precedence and got the 1988-89 confidential report of Bhagwat swiftly expunged. This and other machinations in NHQ and MoD enabled Bhagwat to go to sea as the Eastern Fleet Commander, despite earlier denials by the Naval promotion boards. Bhagwat withdrew his writ petition in what appeared to be a quid pro quo action without consulting the respondents though he had made wide ranging, and serious charges against the Prime Minister, Senior Officers and five Rear Admirals immediately junior to him and others. Ramdas, in 1992, promoted Bhagwat to Vice Admiral against the consensus of the other members of the promotion board which he chaired and Bhagwat stood rejected, graded R in naval terminology. The promotion however was secured via the Ministry of Defence route namely the Defence Secretary and Defence Minister approved the promotion during Prime Minister Narasimha Rao's time. Ramdas fired the gun from the Ministry's shoulders as it were, and he must have had his compulsions .It was common knowledge some senior officers and their wives did not talk to one another civilly but the fine larger Navy took it in its stride for there is semblance of professionalism in this service, as its bedrock. Had there been a Chief of Defence Staff as Arun Singh Committee had recommended, the officer with tri-service responsibility may have offered counsel to the Defence Minister but this task was left to an unqualified Defence Secretary, who is junior to the Chief in rank but wields more clout than the Chiefs. Interestingly Vice Admiral K.K. Kohli as Vice Chief of Naval Staff requested to demit his office a day before Bhagwat took over by going on furlough leave and today his action is seen as an omen of how far matters had gone, and many in the Ministry, should have heeded. Sushil Kumar, the then

Chief of Personnel in 1996, officiated as the Vice-Chief to usher Bhagwat to the high office of CNS.

In the Television interview, Fernandes has quoted Vice Admiral Harinder Singh as having told him that he had pleaded with Bhagwat not to take amiss the fact that he was not in Bhagwat's entourage when he filed the 400 page writ No 2757, and hold it against him. This speaks volumes of what the state between Harinder and Bhagwat was when he took over, even Bhagwat was party to Harinder's promotion to Vice Admiral.

In hind sight it is interesting to recall that in 1996,some days before Admiral Bhagwat took over as CNS, Shri Dilip Karambelkar editor of Mumbai Tarun Bharat filed Public Interest Writ No 1758 on 27 August in the Bombay High Court, quoting verbatim from the Bhagwat's writ of 1990 and challenged the contents of that writ and its withdrawal and questioned whether the other candidates were looked at for the appointment of CNS. The PIL was dismissed, but it is a document of public record and discussed elsewhere. As of today, if Bhagwat is guilty of charges made vehemently public by Minister Fernandes, then the stand of Shri Karambelekar stands vindicated. If not the whole needs immediate legal redressal of the past by the Defence Ministry. Only this review of the past lapses and impartial inquiry into the events of the times will enable a correction of the system and bring back confidence in to the method of progression and selection of higher ranks in the Indian Navy. If not, the ghost of the 400-page writ will haunt the Ministry and the Indian Navy for some time to come.

This chapter is written to explain to readers the back drop of the TV interview as many unaware of the Naval systems and the past did not understand what the charges against Bhagwat were all about and Fernandes was selective in what he disclosed about the murky past in the Ministry of Defence.

The fine Indian Navy with an extremely good and professional track record has seen its reputation tarnished by misdemeanors by its seniors not its fine mid-level officers and men. For no fault of theirs the reputation of the IN has dipped in to the Davy Jones Locker-'Divva Lokka'. The TV interview reveals that the clean white image of the Indian Navy has been sullied not by the fine sailors and above average officers that man the ships and establishments but by the Ministry and squabbling and partisan Admirals who have held the highest offices, who have allowed a Bhagwat to happen in the big white chair in CNS's room in South Block.

SEA POWER, VISHNU BHAGWAT AND THE INDIAN NAVY – AN OVERVIEW

The Bhagwat episode needs to be accompanied by an understanding of the precise function of the Navy and the means by which it achieves its task. What does it do? How does it do it? These are oft-repeated questions of the Indian Navy. In broadest terms in times of war the Navy ensures the Nation the use of the seas around it for transportation of its essentials needs, and denies it to the enemy. It does this by destroying the enemy's naval assets, be they ships, submarines, aircraft or shore-based facilities. A Navy in modern times acts in concert with the other two services to ensure Sea Power - that connotes Command of the seas is exercised and is denied to the enemy. These sentiments and words must remind the nation of the Indian Navy's Stellar role in 1971 war when the newly acquired OSA Class missile boats nick named "Killers" attacked Karachi on 4 Dec 1971 on the Western Seaboard and sank the frigate PNS Khaibar, minesweeper PNS Muhafiz and the freighter Venus challenger with a Chinese crew. On the Eastern seaboard, INS Vikrant's planes attacked East Pakistani build up to ensure that the fine Indian Army was able to secure the Pakistani surrender by General A.K. Naizi to General Arora GoC-in-C Eastern

Command on 16th December 1971. The Indian Navy lost an ASW frigate INS Khukri off Diu on 8 Dec at around 9.30pm when PNS Hangor a Pakistani submarine stalked and torpedoed her. 18 Officers and 176 men went down with their ship. The nuclear task Force 74 of the USA led by USS Enterprise was halted in the Bay of Bengal and it did not have command of the seas and the Indian Navy was able to thwart the US intention to proceed to East Pakistan now Bangladesh.

The Indian Navy operates over, under and on the seas and also safeguards oil installations off the coast. It is composed of fighting and support warships, submarines, aircraft and most important it's highly trained 60,000 fighting men and now women in service. A larger civilian work force mans the dockyards and shore facilities. The Indian Navy has three Commands at Mumbai, Vishakhapatnam and Cochin which the training Command. There are the two Fleets the Eastern and Western and these are the prime fighting arms of the Navy supported by the Flag Officer Naval Aviation at Goa who has all the air assets. Yet fighting is not their daily purpose, it is being prepared to fight and maintain vigil in peace and show the flag abroad. The Navy is the only service that knows no boundaries and freedom of the seas is their heritage. Hence, it has to be very a versatile service and its leaders have to have broad visions as in future energy security and diplomacy is relying more and more on the freedom of the seas.

The twenty years that followed the 1971 war with Pakistani were full of prosperity for the Indian Navy as the strength of the Navy built up to 107 ships including two aircraft carriers INS Vikrant and Viraat, five powerful missile firing Kashin Class Destroyers, 24 frigates, 18 submarines and 92 aircraft. Its morale never ebbed and it gave a good account of itself in foreign cruises, a secret operation in Seychelles, Operation Cactus to restore normalcy in the Maldives in 1989 and in operation Pawan to support the Army. The Navy had converted from a cozy Club that it was, smaller than a corps of the Army, to a full-fledged Service with blue water ambitions. Here in lay a trap for the top echelon, which did not want to delegate powers and be magnanimous. The upright Anglo Indians, Parsis and UK trained officers who had laid the foundations of the Indian Navy were on their last legs and the newer lot were more ambitious and times were a changing. A cadre review held in 1979 led to upgrading of posts with more sanctions. The budget and size of the Navy swelled but the administration of the officers and their reporting system remained unchanged and one commentator has called it incest laden, which is the extreme. The severe competition for early promotions was telling. Much attention was given to the force structure and the naval staff requirements, but training and promotion needs were subject to variety of conflicting demands of branches like aviation and submarines and safe guarding their career prospects .The new breed of professional officers and sailors got exposed to both Soviet and Western equipment and their naval philosophies. The Navy blossomed with a newfound self-confidence and Indian Shipyards also produced wellbuilt warships, at reasonable costs. Weapon systems mainly supplied by Russia were exploited and missile-firing exercises by the Western fleet witnessed by late Admiral Sergei Gorshkov in 1983 even surprised him at the IN's efficiency. The shipyards turned out excellent broad beamed Leanders, smaller missile ships and two HDW submarines from Mazagon Docks, which gave excellent performances even on their first crucial deep dives and weapon firings. Years later in 1998 the Australian Navy has had to order an inquiry on its Collins class submarines which failed deep diving tests and weapon firings. Such was the professional approach to the Navy when the HDW and Bofors Scandals struck the nation and acquisitions became political. The fifth and sixth HDW submarines were not ordered and an LOI on Mazagon Dock was finally issued in 1998 after ten years during Bhagwat's tenure who pushed hard for acquisitions and checked supplies and suppliers with vigil which upset many. The Navy also began to get politicised during Rajiv Gandhi 's time, but the three Service Chiefs of the time weathered operation Brass Tacks and OP Pawan as Army operations per se, but without much cohesion. Instead of agreeing to or pushing for a tri-service Defence structure, better intelligence and procurement, a Chief of Defence Staff system and an integrated Defence Ministry, the Chiefs led by Admiral R.H. Tahiliani Chairman Chiefs of Staff Committee pushed for a Director General Defence Planning Staff in an attempt to cohese the three services. This has proved to be a failure on that score, and has become a posting ground for officers waiting time, for upward progression. The role of this office remains ill-defined and should form part of the National Security Council for results.

Yet in the services there is no balance sheet to judge results. When a management guru was asked what was success in Uniform, he replied it is promotion. This is what Bhagwat fought for in 1990 and is the back drop discussed in the book which seems to have culminated in his removal and the realisation has come that the matters of higher defence need a reorganisation at the Ministry and Inter service levels of operating and cooperation, with a firmer hand on the tilles.

In the Navy internecine battles erupted between the aviators, surface ship captains and submariners and took center stage in the late 80s. With vast powers vested in the Chief of Naval Staff to overwrite reports of all officers and chair all promotion boards for Rear Admirals he was faced with a dilemma to balance all these branches and also ensure his favourites were promoted which at times included his own branch. Each Chief of Naval Staff held a small agenda. From 1987 to 1990 Admirals R.H. Tahiliani and his close confidant and successor Admiral J.G. Nadkarni did some senior level planning but when Bhagwat a professional and a strong proponent of India's need for a powerful Navy got sidelined he fought his way. This story is narrated, as it will affect India's aspirations for sea power, and an understanding of its importance.

When Bhagwat became CNS in 1996 he ambitiously wanted to put his stamp on the Indian Navy and make it more powerful, his way, and aid Indian Shipbuilding as opposed to buying from abroad. He also raised the heckle of arms agents. Admittedly his predecessor Admiral Shekhawat had lamented the neglect of the Navy. Bhagwat over articulated his views and strode stringently over matters of policy, acquisition and personnel, which his PSOs penned as he dictated, to the Ministry. He was over bearing. The Minister and media have quoted widely from notations on file. Bhagwat questioned the spending and the progress of the secret nuclear submarine project called by the misnomer ATV Advanced Technology Vehicle. This project of DRDO needs navy's funding support and in 1979 similar differences arose and Admiral O.S. Dawson deputed Captain Subbarao to audit the design. There were differences of opinion and Subbarao became a pariah for nuclear community at BARC. This did not go down well with the Defence Minister who was unable to control him or resolve matters amicably as communications between the Defence Secretary and the CNS broke down. Fernandes had to take the drastic step of removing the Chief, who was pushing for more sea power for India in the manner he felt right. The Ministry and the Naval Headquarters came into conflict. The Navy has suffered. As of writing there is no serviceable aircraft carrier, modernisation has slipped and the greatest loss will be for naval aviation branch which a potent wing of India's sea power. The acquisition of Gorshkov and the delay in ordering carriers to Cochin Shipyard has figured in the proceedings of Bhagwat.

Indians have to appreciate that as a potential economic power, sea power is one ingredient that cannot be neglected.

THE ART OF BEING AN ADMIRAL - GEORGE BERNARD SHAW

Admiral is a title that has ancient lineage. It originated before the 12th Century from the Muslim Arabs who combined Amir (Commander), the article Al and Bahr (Sea) to make Amir-Al-Bahr. The Civilians shortened it to Amiral and adopted it for naval use. The French copied this title from the Genoese during the seventh crusade (1248-54). The Latin word admirabilis (admirable) may have helped to produce the final which was used by 1620 in England to denote a Commander of Sea going forces. A broad gold stripe with three narrower stripes and a roundel on the uppermost stripe is the insignia of the British, Indian and many other Navies for their Admirals. It is the second highest rank in any Navy. It is full of prestige and is bestowed on the senior most fighting man in the Naval Service. An Admiral of the Fleet the highest is rare, but is an honour accorded to an Admiral who has achieved much and is a life time designation like a Field Marshal and connotes five stars. It is the rank of Admiral that Vishnu Bhagwat achieved on 1 December 1996 and a frank discussion on the art of an Admiral can be eye opening as a backgrounder.

Richart Hough the author of "The Great Admirals" said this to say in 1977. The art of the Admiral has been an unchanging one since Salamis, the ancient sea battle fought in the Mediterranean . He claims only the style of fighting has altered. Nelson, Drake, Kanoji Angre, and Chattrapati Shivaji had to lead boarding parties on to ships in war with swords and later, pistols and muskets. But Admirals Halsey of America, Beatty, Lord Mountbatten, Yamamoto, and Sardari Lal Nanda had to deal with fleets, radar plots, electronic communications, guns, sonars , torpedoes and tactics of task forces and aircraft carriers. More recently Admirals have had to grapple with intense Information Warfare which Admiral Spruance prophetically termed the 'Electronic Brain' in the Second World War.

By the very nature of military affairs, and in absence of war, skill in the profession of arms and national administration of a Navy has to be learnt mostly in theory by studying the science of war and service management, not politics and law , except in cases where it affects a fighting service For this reason great Admirals have always been students of military history and mature leaders . One of the responsibilities of a Commander-in-Chief which an Admiral in the Indian Navy is(because a Chief of Defence Staff system does not exist) is to create an 'atmosphere' as a state of mind in which his staff, his subordinate Principal Staff Officers and Commanders and his ships teams under their captains will blossom in, and work and fight to win. His Navy must know what he wants, they must be given firm guidance and be made aware of the fundamentals of his policy. Inspiration, example and guidance must come from him and permeate the whole force through his commanders. An Admiral needs to be a very clear thinker, able to sort out the essentials from the mass of lesser factors, which bear on every problem and issue, especially some over which he has little or no control. An Admiral must be optimistic and never be petty to hound a brother officer in arms or be chary in allotting praise where it is due. Duke of Wellington when asked if he had to live his life again, what would he do better, said "I should have given more praise". Knowledge and appreciation of computers and computing is now a must in a hi-tech Navy.

The art of the Admiral whether in peace or in war is the art of decision making, of judging odds, alternatives according to his own and other assessments and analysis of his staff. The factors to be taken into include state of material, equipment, readiness, intelligence, quality of morale, political guidance , knowledge of the ability of leaders under him and his feel for his own ability and beliefs. Decisiveness but not brazenness or obstinacy is a supremely valuable quality in an Admiral and procrastination and pettiness is called the thief of success in naval administration and warfare. In India's brief independent history Admiral S.M. Nanda's decisiveness to attack Karachi in the 1971 Bangladesh War in spite of opposition from late the Vice Admiral S N Kohli, was a shining example of Admiralship. Fairness in dealing with all matters is an attribute and so it amounts to the art of keeping your head when all around you are losing theirs. All good Admirals like good Generals or Air Chief Marshals have ensured that they have good scouts (staff officers, well-wishers and informants) and have leaned on their advice when in doubt. Wives and children have played roles in offering counsel, but never over stripping those of his aides and principal staff officers. Admirals have risen to that rank by going through all the rungs of Command in the Navy including attending to functions on ships, establishments and the prestigious Fleet. The Indian Navy has only two Fleets. In the process , the concerned potential Admiral has been judged by his superiors at every stage and the customary confidential reports are the sum of these judgements. An Admiral in a democracy is finally promoted by the political hierarchy and it was Talleyrand who is reported to have said "War is much too serious a thing to be left to military men". Equally it could be said that war is too serious a thing to be left to politicians. The truth is that in modern war and in security functioning of a Nation , the closest cooperation between the politician and the military heads is vital and where it is lacking the desired outcome in war and peace will always be in doubt.

In India this lack of politico military co-operation witnessed in the 1962 India China War, 1965 India-Pakistan War and 1987-90 War in Sri Lanka " OP Pawan" has not been still corrected . In the 1971 War close understanding between General now Field Marshal Sam Manekshaw acting as a Chief of the Three Services, and Mrs Indira Gandhi the Prime Minister was a factor in the success of India's aim and victory . I have dealt with the details of these issues in my book "A Nation and Its Navy at War

(1971)" and "Indians Why We are, What We are (1998)" but in this book the subject is the casualty and analysis of the events leading to the appointment and then the dramatic sacking of "Admiral Vishnu Bhagwat ", when the understanding between the Defence Minister George Fernandes and his head bureaucrat Ajit Kumar and the Navy Chief broke down . The revelations have   disturbed well-wishers of the Navy and the loss is entirely that of the Navy and the Indian Nation . There has been a loss faith in the system of progression   of officers in the Indian Navy. The Admiral who was relieved of his post as Chief of the Naval Staff decided not to fade away as senior retired sailors   should even after he was given his full pension and benefits , but decided to fight his cause and take it into the barracks of the politicians. He has also filed legal affidavits and some interested parties filed Public Interest Litigations . With a shaky coalition government all this was easy and the end is not in sight.

There are golden and dark times for admirals as there are for architects and luck is a factor, not to be under estimated . In the case of Vishnu Bhagwat' he met up with a Defence Minister whose background was that of a Union Leader, and it required true Admiralship to handle him and his senior bureaucrat Mr Ajit Kumar especially as the Prime Minister Atal Behari Vajpayee avoided direct involvement or facing Bhagwat.   The reader should decide if the Admiral was destined to fail or why he failed to succeed. Bhagwat's luck also ran out. Incidentally he was the 13th Chief of the Naval Staff of the Indian Navy.

REMOVAL OF BHAGWAT – THE CHRONOLOGY

At around 5.40 p.m. on Wednesday the 30th December, 1998 two days after he took over as Chairman of the Chiefs of Staff Committee, Admiral Vishnu Bhagwat, Chief of the Naval Staff, whilst in his office, was handed over a cryptic five line order Vice Chief of Naval Staff Vice Admiral P J Jacob signed by his Subir Dutta, Additional Secretary, Ministry of Defence, which said "the President is pleased to withdraw his pleasure of your continuation in office as CNS with immediate effect under Article 310, of the Constitution and Section 15(1) of Navy Act, 1957, due to loss of confidence in your ability to continue as CNS."

Earlier, the same day, a special airplane of RAW was sent to Cochin to fetch Vice Admiral Sushil Kumar for urgent consultation with Raksha Mantri. A nervous Sushil Kumar, uncertain of what was coming entered George Fernandes' office about the same time as the fateful order of dismissal was being served to Admiral Vishnu Bhagwat in CNS' office. The Raksha Mantri warmly congratulated Sushil Kumar on his appointment as CNS with the rank of Admiral. Whether Sushil Kumar hit the roof or not but it was reported that Vishnu Bhagwat on receiving his order collapsed into his chair. Precisely at 5.22 p.m. the new Chief took charge without any fanfare or the presence of the Principle Staff Officers and Vishnu Bhagwat left South Block sans the traditional naval ceremonial farewell. Even the farewell message the outgoing Chief gives to his officers and men was drafted later as he is said to have been unnerved by the suddenness of the thunderbolt of summary dismissal and needed time to collect his thoughts. A history was thus created when a Defence Services Chief was sacked for the first time in independent India in a cloak and dagger style, a manner by which even a peon in the Government cannot be dismissed from service. In a related move, the Defence Secretary Ajit Kumar was transferred to the Department of Industrial Policy and TR Prasad took over as the new Defence Secretary. This was described in Press as an act of cosmetic surgery rather than an acknowledgement of some blame for the sordid events that led to the dismissal of Admiral Vishnu Bhagwat.

The Government said that the services of Admiral Bhagwat, who was to retire in September, 1999, were terminated because he had been taking a series of actions in deliberate defiance of the established system of Cabinet control over the Defence Forces. "The Government is fully conscious of the gravity of such a decision and is aware that it might give rise to uninformed speculation. It is necessary therefore, to clarify that adequate, careful and serious consideration was given to the matter at the highest levels."

"It recognises the need to insulate the Defence Forces so as to preserve their identity, forged over many decades, but deliberate defiance of the Cabinet could not be accepted in any democratic society.

There are a number of cases where democratic countries have had to exercise such a prerogative. Further, there is need to preserve a balance between the interests of national security and the right of the people of this country to be informed of the compulsions which have led the Government to take such a decision. It also needs to be emphasised that in our democratic country, it is the Central Cabinet which has the responsibility of ensuring that our armed forces function effectively, objectively and with their traditional neutrality, within the democratic set-up." The Prime Minister after approving the dismissal of Admiral Vishnu Bhagwat set off for a year-end holiday to the Andamans where he on the following (31 December) evening attended a dinner hosted by Vice Admiral Harinder Singh at his residence.

It was not the first time that Service Chiefs have had conflicts with the bureaucracy or the Ministry of Defence. The first such incident occurred in 1959 when the then Army Chief, Gen. K.S. Thimmayya had put in his resignation on the issue of appointments and promotions of Lieutenants Generals (widely known as B.M. Kaul episode) when his advice was not accepted by the Ministry of Defence. But he subsequently withdrew his resignation after the Prime Minister Jawahar Lal Nehru amicably settled the controversy. There were also problems between Gen. (later Field Marshal) K.M. Cariappa and the political leadership. Not long ago in 1992, MPs led by George Fernandes demanded the removal of the then Army Chief Gen. S.F. Rodrigues for making a statement, 'good governance is not the job of the Army alone' and called some foreign countries 'bandicoots'. He had to apologise to the Government and Parliament for these remarks.

Same evening later at the Navy, House, Admiral Vishnu Bhagwat declined to answer the press representatives' questions and merely said that he had done his duty as a soldier. But his wife Niloufer Bhagwat blamed BJP and Akali Dal's communal politics for her husband's dismissal. She told Rediff on the Net, "the removal of a Service Chief on the reasons put forward by the Government is totally illegal and unwarranted. The PM and RM have behaved like the kings in school book stories who were beheaded for having opposing viewpoints. It is sad and tragic that the PM and RM refused to listen to the rational viewpoints submitted by the Naval Chief and by sacking him on the appointment issues, the Vajpayee Government has violated the Navy Act, 1957." She said that her husband had expected such a decision for some time now but replied to a question that the Admiral would not contest his dismissal in the Supreme Court even though it is illegal and violative of the Constitution. She added that she had all along known that sooner or later she would have to look after him. Since that evening, on the advice of some close friends, she has spoken to the media as the lawyer of Vishnu Bhagwat, rather than his 'bitter' half.

Why the Cloak and Dagger Style of Action by the Government?

The unprecedented style and the secrecy with which the action to dismiss Vishnu Bhagwat and appoint Sushil Kumar as CNS was taken, led a number of analysts to wonder on the need for 'cloak and dagger' method. But the Government being aware of Vishnu Bhagwat's penchant for going to courts and his wife Niloufer being a senior advocate, devised this strategy to close the legal option and ensure that he would not be able to get a 'stay' from the law courts. Issuing the orders for his dismissal and appointing his successor Sushil Kumar simultaneously with latter's physical presence in the South Block did no doubt provide complete surprise and an air of swift surgical operation.

The Reactions from some retired CNS and Senior Officers from other Services.

Admiral R.H. Tahiliami: In his view, the action taken by the Government was terrible and totally unwarranted. The decision showed a total lack of sensitivity towards the morale of the Navy and the other two Services. He felt though that every recommendation made by a Chief to the Government is not binding but the latter cannot force a Chief to accept a Deputy in whom he has no confidence. He placed the major fault at the doorstep of the Government and wondered why the RM did not call Vishnu Bhagwat and Defence Secretary to sort out the differences as discussions in amicable atmosphere can resolve all disputes. According to him the Armed Forces have over the years since independence not demonstrated any ambition to rule the country. India can only be ruled by a democratically elected Government. But the manner of the dismissal of Vishnu Bhagwat would have an adverse effect on the morale of the Defence Services.

Vadm. M.P. Awati: Awati who has known Bhagwat personally from the time he was a Commander felt it was unbelievable that Bhagwat could have done any damage to the Navy and national security. "I would like to know, rather I have a right to know what actions of Bhagwat have damaged the Navy and national security. Vishnu Bhagwat should have been court-martialled and not simply dismissed if the charges of his having endangered national security were true."

Admiral V.S. Shekhawat: He regretted that the entire episode was allowed to go out of hand and it could be handled better by all concerned : the Government as well as NHQ before reaching such an impasse. He dismissed news reports that spoke of the Defence Chiefs feeling neglected or taken for granted. "As CNS, I had no difficulty with any political bosses. Similarly, though we all have our differences and varying perceptions, I don't think defence is particularly peeved with the civilian side. Certainly some people may have more differences and some will have less, but overall, there is nothing which sitting down and talking cannot resolve. Let us always remember that men in such high positions are all very capable and intelligent individuals with their own views." He was emphatic that the Vishnu Bhagwat event would have no bearing on the preparedness of the Defence Forces. "Today we have in place a stable system that can absorb such shocks and upheavals. The sacking concerns only an individual, and his successor is already in place. So on no count, let there be any worry about anyone taking advantage of our problems. An average sailor or officer on the high seas or in coastal bases would not be affected deeply by the Dismissal. This is big news but it has impact only in Delhi, the men on the ships remain busy with their work. An individual's replacement like this, even at the highest level, will have no effect on our defence preparedness." He agreed about the need to recast the defence civilian set-up. "In all democracies, defence is under the politicians, not the bureaucrats. Why should India be any different? "

Admiral J.G. Nadkarni: He has expressed his views in great details on all aspects of the Bhagwat episode. His immediate reaction on 30th December was, "The Cabinet Committee of Appointments is the highest decision making body in the Government. It is headed by the PM. When a Service Chief defies the Cabinet, how can the Government not assert it authority? If the Cabinet's decision was not acceptable to VB, he should have resigned. It was not correct of him not to have implemented the Government's decision for 6 months and depute somebody else of his choice on temporary basis under his own powers. Service officers going to courts has the most serious implications for the Indian Union. What happens if a soldier refuses to go into battle, and wants to take the matter to the Supreme Court? A Government cannot live with attempts to flout its authority." On the question of the adverse effect on the morale of the defence personnel, he has been quite emphatic. "Morale is not a porcelain vase that it can break easily. The average sailor or even a junior officer is not seriously concerned with the office of the CNS or such weighty matters as the Services/Bureaucracy controversy. For all the difference it makes to him, one Chief is like any other. To say that Vishnu

Bhagwat did not refuse to implement the order, he only said that it was 'unimplementable'. Possibly there is a very subtle difference, which only lawyers can understand. As far as the common man is concerned, he is unimpressed by such sea-lawyer language. The Indian Navy is not a High Court. The sailor knows defiance of authority when he sees it. Bhagwat's action was not only not defensible but the situation was getting intolerable. But who is responsible for the Bhagwat fiasco? Primarily the entire event is a failure of the system. For matters to reach such a stage where the only course open to the Government was dismissal of the head of a Service indicates the failure of the promotion system the failure of the appointment system and above all the failure of the selection system for the Chief's post. A large portion of the blame has to devolve on the Government. A critical examination of some events of the past would have revealed certain disturbing traits in Bhagwat's mentality. A detailed examination of the officer's 400 page petition to the Bombay High Court in 1990 should have at least made the Government sit up and carry out an investigation as he had thought fit to tarnish the reputation of a large number of senior officials including the P.M. with his wild allegations. It is well known that the NHQ's promotion board of 1991 which included both the then Chief (Nadkarni) and a future Chief (Ramdas) had not recommended Bhagwat for promotion to the rank of Vice Admiral. He was promoted only after Sharad Pawar, then Defence Minister, intervened."

It may be of interest to read Admiral Nadkarni's recommendation to the Government in October, 1990 on the conduct of Vishnu Bhagwat when he filed a 400 page petition in the Bombay High Court (reported by Manavendra Singh in Indian Express of 6.4.1999). "Bhagwat is a disgruntled officer who is mentally unbalanced. He is schizophrenic and needs psychiatric help. The FOC- in-C Western Command has further informed me that Radm V. Bhagwat has been in the habit of unauthorisedly obtaining and making photocopies of classified official documents for personal use. I am, therefore, of the opinion that the only course that is expedient, speedy and commensurate with the gravity of the misdemeanor of the Flag Officer, is to invoke Article 310 of the Constitution and Section 15(1) of the Navy Act, 1957. I therefore recommend that the Services of Radm V. Bhagwat be immediately terminated under this clause."

That the 'pleasure doctrine' was finally exercised after eight years is the gist of much political football in the country today. History repeats itself, first as a farce and then as tragedy. Bhagwat's case is full of delicious irony and double standards. It is a sordid tale, as much of political manipulation and maneuvering as it is of the denigration of service ethos and character.

"Eventually, the furore over the Bhagwat episode will die down. The sacking will have been worth it if the whole case is examined in detail and lessons drawn from it. Because the next time history will repeat as tragedy."

Analysing the root cause of this unfortunate event, **Maj Gen Ashok Mehta** , a defence analyst alludes to "the failure of the successive governments in meeting the military's long standing demand for greater autonomy and maintaining the sanctity of its chain of command while accepting the principle of civilian political control. Admiral Bhagwat is the first casualty of this proxy war. He dared to question the propriety and legality of political control being hijacked by the civilian bureaucrats. This challenge was perfectly valid, only the methods he employed were questionable. Just to mention two of them – he prepared and disseminated strategic policy papers highly critical of the government and the bureaucracy and went public over his inability to implement the Government orders. It is ironic that the sacking of a Service Chief has come from a BJP-led government that had promised to correct such and other deficiencies in defence policy and personnel management. Admiral Bhagwat had the honourable option of resigning once the Government over-ruled his recommendation. He stuck to his guns on the legal advice of his advocate wife. This was the root of non-compliance of orders. According to one source, Admiral Bhagwat seriously believed that a weak coalition government that dithered for 20 days deciding his case would never dare to sack him, especially since no Service Chief had ever been sacked before. In fact, he had already taken over the additional post of Chairman, Chiefs-of-Staff Committee, albeit without Government clearance."

"The central message of the Bhagwat episode is three fold: (i) the existing higher defence management structures and the chain of command have collapsed; (ii) the Services can no longer tolerate the civilian bureaucratic stranglehold masquerading as civilian political control and the country's courts are getting to have more and more say in military command functions; and (iii) soldiers have just lost faith in the system.

Rear Admiral K R Menon (retired), a close friend of Admiral Vishnu Bhagwat and who writes on strategic affairs, thinks that the real villain of the piece is the bureaucracy in the Ministry of Defence. "The bureaucracy has appointed itself the guardian of the Indian democracy that has to be protected from the armed forces. Over the last 50 years, it is quite clear that if Indian democracy needs protection, it is from the bureaucracy rather than the armed forces, which surely is the last and best surviving institution in the country today."

"The second point is that Bhagwat saw this. Not that the other Chiefs earlier had not, but Bhagwat decided to do something about it. Which is to say that civilian supremacy means the supremacy of Parliament as represented by the Defence Minister, not the supremacy of the civilian bureaucracy. If you conduct a poll among the armed forces middle seniority level and ask them who is the greatest obstacle to the military, they will not say Pakistan, but the bureaucrats. You really have to understand the levels of humiliation suffered by officers who have to get financial sanction for their armed forces. They have virtually to walk files, and very often to bureaucratic officers who are years junior to them, who sit there exercising this power and thinking they are actually defending the country."

"Bhagwat had made it clear that he was not going to accept this system. Bhagwat's contention was that he should be the chief adviser to the defence minister on issues of the country's maritime security. And there should be no ignorant bureaucratic buffers in between."

"During the last one year Bhagwat got together a think-tank at Naval Headquarters and published six policy papers :

- The personnel policy for the navy in the 21st century.

- The technology policy for the navy in the 21st century.

- Information warfare in the 21st century

- The energy security policy of India – the first multi-disciplinary report on the critical   issue   of energy shortage likely to face India in 20 years.

-The soldier and the State, which describes the unwarranted dysfunction between the   Armed forces and the government, caused by keeping the soldier out of government.

-Cry in the wilderness. A compilation of indictment by the parliamentary standing committee of defence, and the parliament estimates committee on the malfunctioning of the defence ministry over a number of years.

" To cap all this, at the Annual Commanders' Conference in October 98, he delivered a stinging speech before the PM and Raksha Mantri stating that a nation with the hierarchy that India possesses will be rapidly shut out of the emerging world competition in the techno-military field. More pointedly, he stated that in national security milieu of the 21st century, a generalist bureaucracy simply has no place anywhere in the security hierarchy of any nation. It suits the civil services to have the public at large, and politicians in particular, believe that the military mind is somewhat dull, hide-bound, hawkish, inflexible and, last but not least, ignorant of subtleties of issues other than the military. They shy away from the suggestion that it is the generalist administration which ceases to grow intellectually, since they undergo very little formalised training, and the major portion of their time is devoted to the technicalities of rules and the dictates of politicians." All this set the bureaucracy of the Ministry of Defence after Bhagwat's blood and intervention in the promotion boards and senior appointments is the handy spanner which the bureaucrats use to tighten screws on any Service Chief.

Lt. Gen. P.N. Hoon: Filed a PIL writ petition questioning the Government's decision. "As members of public we have the right to know why Admiral Bhagwat was sacked. Merely Defence Minister George Fernandes stating the situation was scary and disturbing is not enough. The Government needs to explain why the situation was scary. Was there attempt of a military coup? If that is so, just sacking is not enough. " In a press conference on 5 January in Bombay the General explained, "I am here neither in support of Admiral Bhagwat nor the BJP- led alliance Government. I am only interested in arriving at the truth. Are we living in an era of political dictatorship? If not why is the information denied? The statements by the Prime Minister Atal Behari Vajpayee and the Defence Minister George Fernandes allege a series of defiance of the established structure of democracy, traditional neutrality and objectivity of armed forces, and security concerns, which led to very scary development. All these allegations need to be explained. The only issue of defiance that has appeared openly, is the appointment of DCNS. Does the CCPA believe that the appointment of any individual other than their choice will pose a threat to the Cabinet's control of the Armed Forces or to the national security. The people not only have the right to know, but must act and not remain passive to matters of grave national security, or when the democratic structure appears to be at risk."

The PIL writ petition of Lt. Gen. Hoon was not cleared for hearing by the Bombay High Court on the grounds that the aggrieved individual (Bhagwat) had not been a party to it. A similar PIL Writ filed by Wg Cdr. Sethi in the Delhi High Court also met with the same fate. It has become clear now that unless Vishnu Bhagwat himself files a petition, the courts are not willing to get embroiled with this controversial issue. However, so far Vishnu Bhagwat has publically stated that he has no intention of going to any Court. According to Niloufer, his wife and lawyer, if Bhagwat had gone to the Court it would have limited the issue. Now the issue is open before the country. To this Bhagwat added, "the people of India have to decide who's guilty," a hint that he wanted the issue to be examined and judged by the Parliament.

Comments on the role of Mrs Niloufer Bhagwat

The outbursts of Niloufer Bhagwat to the media in the wake of her husband's dismissal have raised serious question about the propriety of the role of a soldier's wife. TVR Shenoy, noted observer of the political and social scene of the country has succinctly put the feelings of a large section of Indian people by alleging that Admiral Bhagwat is guilty of violating the oath of secrecy that binds every member of the armed forces. Niloufer's proclamation, " the dismissal of Admiral Bhagwat was a political move with wider conspirators involved in the arms supply to the navy. Defence Minister George Fernandes, it seems has fallen for the wiles of 'the arms lobby'." By the evidence of Niloufer Bhagwat herself, it was she who was the repository of his confidences. In doing so Admiral Bhagwat has broken the law as it is a clear dereliction of duty to reveal defence secrets to an unauthorised person. There is a huge difference between the marriage vows and the oaths taken by an officer in the armed forces. Revealing official secrets is a criminal offence and any military man who can't keep his mouth shut is unfit to be a raw recruit, leave alone the Chief of Staff.

Bhagwat kept a deliberate silence from 30th Dec to 14th Jan until he left Delhi and arrived Bombay, his home town that evening in a cavalcade for the last time. His first expression was, "I feel like I have returned home from a long journey." He also promised to "reveal the truth about my dismissal very soon. If supporting the national interest is a crime, then I am guilty. I have done my duty and followed the Constitution and I am proud of that. His wife and lawyer Niloufer said, "An honest officer who was selected for his secular values has been victimised by a fascist Government. Bhagwat described the allegations of the Government as a "tissue of lies" and said that he will not allow these lies and slander to pass. At the Mumbai Airport he issued a prepared statement which said," When I was relieved of my charge, I decided not to challenge the Government, in spite of the grave injustice done to the Navy. However, I will not allow my honour to be besmirched in this manner. I have given my whole life to the Navy and the nation and I am proud of the legacy I am leaving behind as a loyal and patriotic soldier of the Republic. I have done my duty. I have thought of what Lokmanya Tilak said when he faced trial for sedition in colonial India. There is a higher power that rules the destiny of men and nations and it may be the will of providence that the cause which I represent may prosper more by my sufferings than remaining free."

The Compromise Formulae

Every thinking man has wondered as to why the Government did not try to find other alternative via-media to get over the fractitious Bhagwat issues rather than take the unprecedented course of summary dismissal. Unconfirmed reports allude to two such courses which were tried by the MOD. One was sometime in Sep/Oct 98 when Bhagwat was sounded to put in his resignation in lieu of an ambassadorial assignment. This was straight away declined by Bhagwat saying that such a thing he would consider after laying down his office. The other was about the appointment of Vadm Harinder Singh. It was suggested to Bhagwat that let both Harinder and Madanjeet (Appointed as DCNS temporarily by Bhagwat under CNS' powers) be taken out of reckoning for the post of DCNS and appointed elsewhere and a third person be made the Deputy Chief. Harinder was slated to become the Director General, Coast Guard in Delhi. Bhagwat initially agreed to this proposal but after a day or two rescinded. It was on this back-stepping that George Fernandes is reported to have blown his head and started the chain of action to relieve Bhagwat of his office under the 'pleasure doctrine'.

Steps to Reorganise Ministry of Defence

On 5 January, Defence Minister George Fernandes announced that before the end of the month, the Services Headquarters will be integrated into the Defence Ministry. A few days later, after the three Services had made presentations on the subject, he constituted a Group to work out the details of "restructuring of the Services and their integration with the Ministry of defence. If the Services are integrated with the Defence Ministry and get a greater say in policy-making, then perhaps the controversy created by Bhagwat's dismissal will not have gone in vain.

Fernandes also confirmed on 14 April '99 that MOD is working on the creation of an "internal" tribunal without any bureaucrat being member of it which will function as the last point of call for any serviceman with a promotion, appointment or a posting grievance. This Tribunal will function within the structure of an integrated MOD and would have necessary legal and administrative authority to decide on all statutory complaints and redressal of grievances. The Army, Navy and Air Force Acts will be suitably amended through the Parliament.

The Political Fall-out

The first political salvo was fired by the Janata Party leader Subramanian Swamy on 4 Jan 99 demanding a judicial commission of enquiry to probe into the sacking of the Naval Chief, Adm Bhagwat. He said the Commission should be headed by a sitting Supreme Court judge and should probe all aspects that resulted in the dismissal of an Admiral, first time in Indian history. The decision of the BJP-led government was very unfortunate and unwarranted and held Prime Minister Atal Behari Vajpayee and Defence Minister George Fernandes responsible for the incident. Swamy also suggested that a Committee of former Admirals who have retired in the last 20 years, be constituted to examine the matter and its consequences in detail.

It did not take long for the political parties in opposition to realise the crucial importance and potency of the Bhagwat affair in undermining the stability of the BJP-led coalition Government of Shri Atal Behari Vajpayee. Each one did its home-work and calculated the political mileage that could be gained in making this matter a cause for show-down in the forthcoming budget session of the parliament. By coincidence or design, Bhagwat travelled from Bombay to Delhi and broke his formal silence on the circumstances of his dismissal and self-imposed seclusion at a meeting with the media in the Press

Club on 22 February. He denied all allegations put forth by the Government sources as well as levelled charges of wrongdoings upon the Defence Minister, George Fernandes. The focus of allegations against Bhagwat was that during his tenure as the Navy Chief he had violated norms of personnel policy. He had protected a senior officer handling naval logistics matters despite reports of serious financial malfeasance against him. He had committed breach of security about a top secret naval project and had also 'tampered' with the annual confidential reports (ACRs) of subordinate officers he was not favourably disposed towards. Of course, defiance of the authority of the Cabinet in not implementing the CCPA's decision of appointing Vice Admiral Harinder Singh as the Deputy Chief of Naval Staff was the most obvious one. After this 'meet the press' the newspapers had a daily fare of delicious news, news-leaks and views from all and sundry either in favour or against Vishnu Bhagwat and it became quite clear that the Parliament would also have its more than due share of what the PM described as the 'Bhagwat Purana'.

After the initial preoccupation of the parliament with the situation in Bihar and over the question of the President's rule there, the Vajpayee Government having proved its majority in the Lok Sabha but withdrew the Ordinance in the face of the sure defeat in the Rajya Sabha, the Vishnu Bhagwat issue became the centre-piece of the proceedings in both the Houses. The opposition with Congress party in lead demanded discussion on this issue before commencing the debate on the budget presented on 27 February. On 4 March, Prime Minister called in leaders of all the major parties in the Rajya Sabha to explain why a debate on the Bhagwat issue was inadvisable. After initiating the discussion, he sat in silent solidarity whilst Fernandes read out select extracts from confidential files. Parliamentarians were not given the privilege of examining the documents themselves on grounds of their sensitivity. The purpose of this exercise was to provide the MPs with a hint of the grave national interests that were supposedly threatened by Bhagwat. The further stand taken by the opposition parties reflected that the MPs were not convinced and a demand for a Joint Parliamentary Committee to go into the matter was raised.

The Government remained unyielding for a while but it became apparent that the opposition members were not prepared to concede that the unprecedented dismissal of a Service Chief merited the waiver of parliamentary scrutiny on grounds of national security. As prospect of a paralysis of parliamentary business loomed, a more generous-sounding offer was made by the Government side that the presiding officers of the two Houses would constitute an informal committee drawn from both the Treasury and Opposition benches, to examine the relevant material and determine whether a debate would be appropriate. Though initially to have found general favour, the confidence of the Opposition in the proposed mechanism plummeted on account both of the procedure adopted and the composition of the committee. Within the Congress(I), Sharad Pawar seemed inclined to give the committee a chance to function but his view was not shared by any other leader of substance both of his own party and that of the others.

On 16 March, Congress(I) MP, Rajesh Pilot raised the matter in the Lok Sabha, claiming knowledge of a sworn affidavit which Bhagwat had filed in which he had pointed out certain gross abuses of power by the Defence Minister. On the following day George Fernandes dismissed the Bhagwat affidavit as a scurrilous and self-serving document and at a meeting of the informal committee, he accepted the demand for a discussion in both Houses with the parameters of the debate being set by the inherent sense of restrain of the members. The opposition, however insisted that the discussion should not be routine or cursory in nature and should be followed by a vote in both Houses on the conduct of the Government. After days of acrimony, the parliament went into its mid-session recess on March 19 with the matter unresolved. The Lok Sabha would discuss the matter on April 15 while the date for Rajya Sabha is yet to be fixed.

By allowing a parliamentary debate on the Bhagwat affair, the Government seemed to have chosen the lesser of the two evils, the other option being the quasi-judicial parliamentary inquiry (JPC). Media analysts also surmised that the Bhagwat affair will not stop at Parliament but would go to the courts which after all might be the purpose of the 51 page affidavit that Bhagwat had prepared and copies of which are reported to be in the hands of the Press as well as favourable politicians. Prem Shankar Jha has opined in March 29 issue of 'Outlook', " Bhagwat has every right to demand that serious allegations for which he was summarily dismissed be sustained in a court of law. But even otherwise the courts will have to decide whether the Government can dismiss a serving Chief summarily without inquiry or court-martial, upon suspicion alone. It will also have to decide whether civilian authority is equipped to determine, entirely on its own, that a breach of security has indeed taken place and mete out such summary punishment, or whether this is not an encroachment by the executive upon the preserve of the judiciary." The Bhagwat saga seemed to have just begun.

Jayalalitha Fires the Bhagwat Missile

The ADMK leader Jayalalitha with her 18 MPs in the BJP-led coalition Government has been a very difficult partner ever since its formation in March 1999. Her list of unsavoury demands has been endless and a constant threat to the stability of this Government. Whether her behaviour is the manifestation of the pique against the BJP leadership whom she has accused of trying to break her Party or the more personal frustration due either to BJP's inaction over stalling the court cases of corruption against her filed by the Karunanidhi's DMK government in Tamilnadu or her demand to bring down the latter and impose President's rule there is a matter of specualation . On the evening of 3 April Jayalalitha gave an ultimatum to Vajpayee that unless he favourably responded within a reasonable time to her demands of dismissing George Fernandes from the Miinistry, reinstatement of Vishnu Bhagwat as the Naval Chief and a probe by a JPC into corruption charges against George Fernandes levelled by Bhagwat, she would withdraw support from the present Government. Prima facie, her demands appeared rather tall and 'unimpementable' by the BJP leadership despite the formers threat to attach the engine of her support to some other train in Delhi.

George Fernandes' reaction to Jayalalitha's demands was, " Why should I resign ? The Prime Minister has not asked me to. Prime Minister Vajpayee confirmed once again, "We are ready for a debate over Bhagwat's dismissal as well as charges of corruption being levelled by Bhagwat against George Fernandes. Defending her sack George demand Jayalalitha pointed out that Bhagwat was sacked without even being issued a show-cause notice. "We are perfectly justified in demanding dismissal of Fernandes." While the Ministry of Defence put its mind to picking holes in Bhagwat's affidavit against George Fernandes, K. Subrahmanyam, former Secretay Defence Production, Director Institute of Defence Studies and Analyses and presently the convener of the National Security Advisory Board denied statements made by Bhagwat in his affidavit in regard to Fernandes having links with foreign intelligence agencies and had as Minister of Industries in the first Janata Government (1987) advised the Cabinet to switch over to Western arms purchases in toto and stop all supplies from the then USSR, and these points were either conveyed or corroborated to Bhagwat by Subrahmanyam who has to the media categorically affirmed, "I never raised or discussed these with Bhagwat for the simple reason that I had no way of knowing any of this. In my personal capacity I had no access to this kind of information, so there is no question of confirming this to Bhagwat on my part."

The rift between BJP-led Government and its AIDMK partner continued to widen and the two ministers of Jayalalitha's party resigned from the Cabinet. The battle line seemed to have been drawn with all sorts of possibilities before and after the fall of the Vajpayee Government. Aware of the public dismay over the charges against him and the cloud over the reasons for the dismissal of Bhagwat, George Fernandes went to the electronic media and gave oneand half hour interview to Karan Thapar on all matters of import before and after the Bhagwat affair.

The Fall of Vajpayee Government

Jayalalitha arrived Delhi on the evening of 12 April harbingering dark clouds over the fate of Vajpayee's Govt and intense politiking for winning the numbers game. Amidst uncertainties of what would happen if the Vajpayee Govt fell, She met the President on the morning of 14 April just a day before the reconvening of the Parliament and conveyed to him her party's withdrawal of support to the BJP-led Coalition Govt. The President asked Vajpayee to seek a vote of confidence in his Govt on the floor of the House after the commencement of the session without laying down a time limit. However, Vajpayee moved a motion of confidence on the very morning of the reconvening of parliament session on 15 April thus throwing the gauntlet in a do or die situation. There was an intense debate with frequent slanging matches between the Treasury and the Opposition benches with Bhagwat affair being hardly mentioned as the core issue. Whilst the debate went on till 5-30 AM on 17 April morning, efforts were being made behind the scenes to garner support of small parties by both sides as it was clear that the fight was neck to neck. Around 2 PM after the voting was done, it turned out that the Vajpayee Govt lost the confidence of the House by just one vote - 270 vs 269. One wondered whether the reasons for the dismissal of Bhagwat would also be as close in the ultimate reckoning if it were to be ever done in an open manner. Did Bhagwat's sunken ship take the Vajpayee's Government down with it? Only the future events would confirm - for individuals are just pawns on the political chess board in the hand of the big players. !!

Chronology of Events Leading to and post Dismissal of Admiral Vishnu Bhagwat

Buildup of Controversies

Nov 9 '97 - NHQ sent a file recommending officers for the posts of Vice Chief and Cs-in-C of three Commands at Kochi, Vishakhapatnam and Mumbai. The Defence Secretary took two months to send the file for approval to the Minister. In contrast Mulayam Singh took only 48 hours to clear the names. The file went to the PMO but was withdrawn on Jan 25 '98 by the Cabinet Secretary. It came back to Bhagwat with a request that the appointments of Flag Officers be changed. Bhagwat didn't concur and returned the file with his explanation. Mulayam again agreed with Bhagwat and sent the file to the Cabinet Secretary for presentation to the ACC. Nothing further happened till Bhagwat met the PM, I.K. Gujral in end Feb and the latter appreoved the appointments. By going to the PM, Bhagwat had tweaked Ajit Kumar's nose who thereafter got even by sitting on all key issues raised by NHQ. Thus, when NHQ reported how a senior MOD official on an arms purchase mission in Russia had been caught in a classic honeypot operation, Kumar "lost" the file.

Feb '98   -   Acting upon military intelligence rather than that of RAW, the Navy intercepted three trawlers in Bay of Bengal carrying arms for two insurgent groups in Assam and one in Myanmar. This caused immense anger in RAW, which had been funneling weapons to insurgents in Myanmar.

May 29-30 '98   -   The confrontation that completed the rift between Bhagwat and Fernandes came after the Navy intercepted two more Thai trawlers near Narcodam Island in the Andamans. When the trawlers attempted to flee to Burmese waters, the Navy sank one of them and from the other it recovered arms and 50 kg of heroin.

Jul 27 '98   -   The Defence Secretary issued an order barring the Service Chiefs from "acting on intelligence reports ... relating to gun-running and other illegal activities in the Andaman Sea without prior approval."

Aug 8 '98   -   At an NCC function attended by all three Service Chiefs, Bhagwat told George Fernandes that the said order was virtually unenforceable. There were two other operations, one off Sri Lanka, the other off west coast aimed at intercepting arms supply to insurgents. Bhagwat did not see why only one of the three operations should be subject to clearance by the Ministry. He also said the fear that the Navy might cause a diplomatic row by entering Myanmar's waters during a chase was bogus because the operation was being carried out in cooperation with Myanmar authorities.

28 Aug '98 - Grorge Fernandes wrote to the PM for the first time apprising him of the damage being done by Bhagwat to national security and his defiance of civil authority.

Bhagwat called by the Principal Secretary to PM, Brijesh Mishra and cautioned by him to take care. Bhagwat thereafter met the Defence Minister to ask why he had written such letter to the PM.

08 Sep '98 - All three Services Chief sent a letter to the Defence Minister complaining about " a negative and unsupportive attitude" of Ajit Kumar, the Defence Secretary.

Oct '98 - At the inauguration of the Annual Navy Commanders Conference with the PM and the Defence Minister present, Bhagwat delivered a stinging speech on the role of the civilian bureaucracy in MOD.

05 Nov '98 - George Fernandes wrote second time to the PM citing more examples of Bhagwat stepping out of line specifically in connection with a Top Secret project.

Controversy over Vice Admiral Sushil Kumar's appointment/representation

Aug 14 '98 - Vice Admiral Sushil Kumar C-in-C South sent his first representation to Adm Bhagwat for posting to an operational Command (Mumbai or Vishakhapatnam).

14 Sep '98 - Vice Addmiral Sushil Kumar sent his second representation to Adm Bhagwat.

22 Sep '98 - Vice Admiral Sushil Kumar sent his third representation to Adm Bhagwat.

29 Sep '98 - Knowing as a former Chief of Personnel that a letter to CNS was not a statutory complaint, the first such complaint to NHQ.

07 Oct '98 - Vice Admiral Kumar sent his second statutory complaint to NHQ.

30 Oct '98 - Vice Admiral Kumar verbally agreed to withdraw his statutory complaint after a meeting with CNS in his office and to abide by the CNS' decision. Bhagwat called the VCNS and CinC Western Command in his office and Kumar repeated what he'd earlier said to CNS and thereafter the latter made a notation on the file.

24 Nov '98 - Vice Admiral Kumar sent his statutory complaint to the Defence Minister directly with copy to CNS.

27 Nov '98 - Vice Adm Kumar rang up George Fernandes in panic begging for protection as Bhagwat had threatened him with disciplinary action over the

phone.

30 Nov '98 - Admiral Bhagwat wrote to Vadm Kumar, " since your first statutory complaint is dated Oct' 7, it is incorrect to claim an application dated Aug' 14 ... can be treated as ... as your first statutory complaint. Accordingly your addressing the Raksha Mantri on 7 Oct and your latest direct representation ... are violative of provisions of the Regulations, Navy, and are therefore actionable."

07 Dec '98 - Fernandes wrote third time to the PM about how Bhagwat had lied to him regarding Vadm Sushil Kumar's representation and threatened him with disciplinary action.

Controversy over Vice Admiral Harinder Singh's appointment

Feb '96 - Promotion Board of which Bhagwat was a member considered Harinder Singh eminently suitable in all respects for promotion to the rank of Vice Admiral and was duly promoted

May '97 - Harinder Singh visited Russia and the UK on leave after duly informing C-in-C East of the details of this visit.

Nov '97 - No adverse comments in Harinder Singh's ACR.

18 Dec '97 - Harinder Singh wrote to Bhagwat on his grievance for not being considered for transfer to NHQ as a PSO.

23 Mar '98 - Harinder Singh sent his 'Redressal of Grievances' letter to C-in-C Eastern Command, his immediate superior. Bhagwat made adverse entries in Harinder Singh's ACRs of Nov '97 and Nov '98.

04 Apr '98 - Bhagwat appointed Vadm Madanjeet Singh as DCNS under his own powers.

30 Apr '98 - NHQ issued a show-cause notice to Harinder Singh for his offending remarks in the ROG letter.

Harinder Singh moved Calcutta High Court to quash the 'show-cause notice'.

23 Jun '98 - Calcuttta High Court directed MOD/NHQ to remove the adverse remarks from Harinder Singh's ACRs and consider his request for a PSO's appointment on merit /seniority as per rules.

12 Aug '98 - MoD ordered all adverse remarks by Bhagwat in Harinder Singh's ACR to be expunged at the direction of Calcutta High Court.

17 Aug '98 - Harinder Singh sent his formal reply to NHQ's show-cause notice with unqualified apology for his alleged offensive remarks.

28 Aug '98 - Bhagwat as CNS filed an affidavit in Calcutta High Court with allegations against Defence Secretary etc

9 Dec '98 - ACC overruled Bhagwat's

recommendation for DCNS and appointed Vadm Harinder Singh to the post.

Bhagwat contended that ACC's order was 'unimplementable' as it violated the Navy Act.

The Final Action

Dec '98 - Fernandes wrote a 20 page letter to the ACC listing grounds for Bhagwat's dismissal.

28 Dec '98 - Cabinet Committee on Security Affairs decideed on dismissal of Bhagwat and formalised the change of guard viz appointment of Vadm Sushil Kumar as CNS.

Dec 29 '98 - Bhagwat took over as the Chairman of Chiefs of Staff Committee from Air Chief Marshal Sareen without a formal Govt order/approval.

Dec 30 '98 - Bhagwat summarily removed from office of CNS.

Political Fall-out

4 Jan '99 - Janata Pary Leader Subramanian Swamy demanded a judicial commission of enquiry to probe into the sacking of Adm Bhagwat.

14 Jan '99 - Bhagwat gave a formal statement to the media on reaching Mumbai in which he described the allegations of the Govt as 'tissue of lies' which he would not allow to pass and promised to reveal the truth very soon.

16 Jan '99 - Sharad Pawar the Congress leader of Loksabha stated that the full facts of Bhagwat affair need to be known.

22 Feb '99 - Bhagwat met the media at the Press Club in Delhi and levelled charges against George Fernandes. This led to charges and countercharges being published daily in the Press for and against Bhagwat.

23 Feb '99 - Parliament's budget session began but remained busy with first the presentation of the Budget and then with the question of the President's rule in Bihar.

04 Mar '99 - PM and Defence Minister briefed leaders of the major opposition parties in Rajyasabha on the reasons for the dismissal of Bhagwat.

09 Mar '99 - Opposition raked up Bhagwat issue to nail the Govt and demanded it to come clean on the affair.

10 Mar '99 - Army Chief Gen Malik refuted Bhagwat's charges and termed them 'irrational'.

11 Mar '99 - ' facts hidden from Parliament' – Bhagwat's dismissal a ' political' strategem, said Communist Party leader Indrajit Gupta, whilst Govt blowed hot and cold.

Mar '99 - Govt agreed to the formation of an informal committee to examine the material and determine whether a debate would be appropriate.

12 Mar '99 - Opposition turned down the offer for an informal examination beacause of disagreement over the composition of the committee as also the procedure. The demand for an examination by a Joint Parliamentary Committee (JPC) raised in addition to the discussion in the Parliament.

13,14 & 15 Mar '99 - The proceedings in the parliament stalled by opposition parties with Congress in the lead pressing for a discussion on the Bhagwat affair and appointment of a JPC.

16 Mar '99 - Rajesh Pilot, of Congress(I) raised the matter of a debate in the Parliament again and claimed the knowledge of a sworn affidavit prepared by Bhagwat in which he had made allegations of aiding gun-running for the insurgents, supporting the arms dealers and their commission agents and abuse of powers against George Fernandes.

17 Mar '99 - George Fernandes refuted Bhagwat's allegations and conveyed the readiness of the Govt to have a discussion in both Houses of Parliament but without voting on the issue.

18 Mar '99 - Opposition insisted on its demand for discussion followed by vote and a JPCto go into the matter. The parliament went into mid-session recess from19 Mar with the matter remaining unresolved and to be taken up again on 15 Apr on recommencement of the session.

27 Mar '99 - Ms Jayalalitha, leader of AIADMK Party and an ally of BJP-led Govt demanded an enquiry into Bhagwat's dismissal and his allegations against the Defence Minister at the Coalition's Co-ordination Committee's meeting.

03 Apr '99 - Jayalalitha gave ultimatum to Vajpayee of withdrawing support unless George Fernandes was removed as Defence Minister and Bhagwat reinstated as CNS.

O5 Apr '99 - Two AIADMK ministers to resign from Vajpayee Govt.

09 Apr '99 - Jayalalitha pulled AIADMK Party out of Coalition Co-ordination Committee.

14 Apr '099 - Jayalalitha met the President and conveyed her withdrawal of support to the Vajpayee Govt. President asked Vajpayee to seek confidence vote in the Loksabha.

15 Apr '99 - Parliament's session reconvenes and Vajpayee moved a motion of confidence for his Govt.

17 Apr '99 - After two days of intense and heated debate on the confidence motion, Vajpayee Govt lost by one vote – 270 against vs 269 for the motion.

POTRAIT OF GEORGE FERNANDES

George Fernandes, the well-known spectacled labour leader, with a mop of tousled grey hair, invariably clad in khadi kurta-pyjama even on most formal occasions, was born on 3rd, June 1930 in Mangalore, which is now in Karnataka. His long rough and tough political career was spent in Bombay leading trade unions in Bihar with the Mafia amongst others and in New Delhi opposing the Nehru Congress family dynastic rule with dogged stances from the opposition benches. He took over as India's thirtieth Defence Minister on the 20th of March 1998 in the BJP coalition Government and is the President of the Samata party, which has 5 members in the Lok Sabha though Kalpanath Rai has deserted him. Mrs. Jaya Jaitley, a close associate and friend of George, is the Secretary of the Samata party. Fernandes has had a rich but brief experience of being the Minister of Communications, Industry and Railways and so he knows what Ministership is all about when he took office. He was no green horn when he took over defence, but it must be remembered he berated General Rodrigues when he made the statement that good governance was also the Military's responsibility, and George extracted an apology. His present term as Defence Minister was thirteen months long and he sacked the 13th Chief of Naval Staff and that act will haunt him for a long time to come. It contributed to the fall of the BJP Government. He went on TV nationwide, in mid-April, for full 90 minutes, to explain his reasons for acting the way he did, for which earlier he had said he felt miserable, but a poll showed the nation was not fully convinced. As a journalist put it, George is always on the wrong side of the establishment, and his tenure in 1998-99 in the Government will go down as the most controversial in management terms. He has not been able to explain his action against Bhagwat cogently and has hidden behind the fig leaf of National Security while dismissing a Chief in a coup like operation. He also drew small swords with the Air Chief Marshal S.K. Sareen, the ex-Chief of Air Staff, who accused the Ministry for not defending him against charges in the media, and also riling up the Shantushti shopping complex issue which is still to be resolved between the Air Force Wives Welfare Association and the MOD.

Many indications are that Fernandes used his Defence Secretary Ajit Kumar and the Director of Defence PR to fire his many guns, and so in the bargain much dirty linen on arms dealings especially about Crown Corporation and a company called Makalu which supplied Navy spares has been aired in the media. The name of Rear Admiral S. Poruhit also been figured, has been aired in the media. Some is fact some is fiction and the problem began when Rajiv Gandhi banned arms agents, which in reality is not feasibility.

George has faced charges of being a supporter of the LTTE by Jayalalitha and others, harbouring Burmese dissidents and conniving to permit supply of arms at times flow to the North East area of India but he has always taken such charges in his stride with alibis. The Burmese students who live with him were picked up on his way to Parliament, he has stated on TV, and a relief agency pays for them and so claims innocence. But, is it proper to house aliens in Government accommodation? He denies the LTTE connection. He has spoken a lot about an Inter service Operation Leech in the Andamans. It was a boched up operation and reads like the Samba case, where one side the Defence officials did not know what the intelligence agencies were doing and innocents got embroiled. Bhagwat has gone on record to ask that reports of the personal dossiers of Fernandes available with the Intelligence Bureau and RAW, which are routinely kept on important personalities be bared along with his. As Fernandes has been named in the Baroda Dynamite case to blow up railway tracks and union activities there are bound to be dossiers at least of the past. If that happens it will be historic to release such data which every nation guards to the hilt, because it is privileged information for good governance, and not for public disclosure.

In August 1998 Fernandes as the Chief guest came to the NCC Annual games opening Ceremony March Past at the Jawahar Lal Nehru Stadium over twenty minutes late and did not utter a word of apology for keeping the 1500 cadets, VIPs including the Chiefs waiting. As commentator for the event I kept the crowds amused and when I asked his aide if I could offer an innocuous apology on his behalf. He said this Minister has no reason to apologise, he is a very busy man and the crowd should understand. He is the only

Minister not to have inaugurated a Commander's Conference because of pre occupation with political matters. That sums up tenacious George who believes all he does is right. In Military matters Tradition and pomp are an essential ingredient which again he abhors. He was unable to check Bhagwat, so he sacked him.

His political stances and directives have always raised hackles but in the end he has won and he may get away in the Bhagwat case too. He voted to banish Coca-Cola from India and it did come to pass. As Shastri Ramachandran in Times of India (TOI) stated he called businessmen and captains of industry rats and got away with it. As a trade unionist he mobilised hotel workers and taxi drivers in Mumbai and kept many employers on the run. He was called the giant-killer who humbled S.K. Patil as leader of the railway strike, which led to the emergency and he went to jail, handcuffed. He got elected to Parliament from jail by one of the biggest margins ever and has served seven terms in Parliament. He is a staunch socialist. He has always displayed a pathological aversion to the Congress even before the emergency. It is written of him, George could not be beaten into submission, despite the atrocities inflicted on him and his family. He is married to Late Humayun Kabir's (Secretary of education under Maulana Abdul Kalam Azad) daughter and has a son by her.

George occupied the South Block office which was vacated by the Lucknow trotting Hindi speaking Defence Minister Mulayam Singh Yadav. He came armed with the reputation of a 'no nonsense' English speaking fire brand 'gung ho' Union Leader, who had stormed into offices of corporations, stood for

Tibet's independence and cared little for Chairmen of companies and had shifted alliances from one political party to another. He is known to have deserted Morarji Desai for Charan Singh and so came with a reputation of being a shifty character in the political arena. This can be an asset in politics but in Defence when on says something it or gives an order there is no shifting sands about it or the Military edifice will crumble. When asked once to inaugurate and start a new train he quipped he knew better how to stop trains. His personal views on defence before assuming office included an anti-nuclear policy stance and were termed a peacenik. One wonders whether he knew he would be made responsible to steer India's Defence in to the nuclear haves camp after Pokhran II and one wonders how his conscience took it. Bhagwat swears Brajesh Misra of the PMO told the Chiefs a few days before the nuclear explosions of May 1998 not to disclose a word about the forthcoming tests to Fernandes and it has not been denied directly. If this were true then there is something amiss in how the Defence Minister and the Prime Minister's office functioned on such delicate issues of National security and the lie in the matter needs to be pinned. The Navy earlier knew him as one who had discussed labour matters in dockyards in Mumbai and Cochin and the Navy has had an excellent record of uniformed and civilian workers executing their roles in Dockyards. In the Defence Ministry it was immediately evident he had limited background of weapons, military history, strategy and defence management and yet was keen to learn but his political role as the mediator for the BJP party kept him busier more with politics, that the Ministry. He did push bureaucrats to visit Siachen, Submarines and the Rajasthan desert in summer and promised to reform the Defence Ministry. He personally visited Siachen thrice and gained much popularity. Time only will tell how much he achieved during his period in office and in the post-Bhagwat period.

THE STORY OF VICE ADMIRAL HARINDER SINGH AND HIS REQUEST TO BE CONSIDERED FOR A PSO POST

The story of Vishnu Bhagwat took another interesting turn in 1998 when Bhagwat as CNS tried to play down Vice Admiral Harinder Singh ostensibly for some old cudgels and opinions he had of this officer, whom he had cleared in the Promotion board to become a Vice Admiral in 1996. He gave this senior officer an adverse report . Just as Bhagwat in 1990 desired to become the Fleet Commander and put in his statutory request and then go to court, Harinder a smart professional officer did the same when his request to become a Principal Staff Officer was not being acceded to by Bhagwat who gave him an adverse report for staying with an ex naval officer and his old friend in Moscow because they had some connections with arms supplies. Harinder objected to the adverse report went to court in a writ and got redress through the court to get the Ministry of Defence to expunge the report . The ministry did this without recourse to the CNS and this angered Bhagwat. Mrs. Bhagwat filed a unique Contempt Petition in the Calcutta High Court against Vice

admiral Harinder Singh, The Defence Minister ,
Defence Secretary Mr. Ajit Kumar in his official and
private capacity and the Joint Secretary Navy Mr. R P
Bagai . It was unprecedented and on 5 November
1998 the petition was rejected in limine. The MOD
pamphlet is reproduced in parts along with the
judgement to unfold another part of the episode in
which Vice Admiral Harinder Singh was cleared by
the ACC to become the DCNS on 9 December 1998
and Bhagwat told the Government that it was
unimplementable.

Allegation: Vice Admiral Harinder Singh had
close relation with the Defence Minister. Insinuations
have also been made special favours were shown to
him because of his links with arms dealers and
because of the influence of Akali Dal leaders.

Truth: Much has been made of the information
reportedly given by ex-Chief of Naval Staff about the
activities of arms peddlers and several naval officials'
involvement with the same. The ex-Chief of Naval
Staff knows only too well that procurement of any
equipment takes place only after the case is proposed
and recommended by the Naval Headquarters. As
Chief of Naval Staff he had total control over all
kinds of procurement. If he had noticed or was aware
of any wrongdoing, corruption or irregularities he
could have and in fact should have taken firm and
effective action against such officers. He could have
further referred to the Government specific charges
and instances, for investigation by the CBI or for
approving exemplary disciplinary action like removal
from service dismissal, etc. However, all that he did

was to make adverse entries in the ACRs of a few officers which would not have even come to the notice of the Ministry, leave alone the Raksha Mantri, but for the statutory representations filed by them and the directives issued by a Court the Government to address these matters. The Courts issued such directives only because as the Chief of Naval Staff Admiral Vishnu Bhagwat chose to sit on these statutory representations. The charge levelled against Vice Admiral Harinder Singh through the rather indirect method of making an entry in his ACR was that he had enjoyed the hospitality of a retired naval officer who is alleged to be working for an arms company.

In this case, it needs to be stated at the outset that the Ministry of Defence processed his case only because of an explicit direction of the Calcutta High Court that the Ministry of Defence alone shall dispose of this matter. It was observed in response to the allegations against Vice Admiral Harinder Singh pertaining to his having enjoyed the hospitality of a retired Naval officer that he had submitted in his explanation that the said retired officer had been his childhood friend, they had been brought up together, they were also course mates in NDA and had been colleagues in the Navy. The officer had further clarified that if he had anything to hide or was engaged in any improper activity, he would not have voluntarily the Naval Attaché in Moscow about his place of stay during his trip to Moscow. The officer had been issued a show cause notice for having used strong language. Viewed in the backdrop of the submissions made by the officer it was observed in the Ministry that the language used was indicative of his anguish against what he perceived as an attempt being made by the Chief of Naval Staff to harm his career. In view of the unqualified apology tendered by Vice Admiral Singh and in the context of the clarifications given by him, it was deemed appropriate to accept his explanation. The sequence of events in this case will clearly demonstrate the bias on the part of Admiral Vishnu Bhagwat.

i) Promotion Board February 1996 where Vishnu Bhagwat as FOC-in-C Western Command was member (other members being Chief of Naval Staff, Admiral V.S. Shekhawat as Chairman, Vice Admiral P.S. Das, FOC-in-C Eastern Command as member, Vice Admiral A.R. Tandon, FOC-in-C Southern Command as member, Vice Admiral R. Kohli, VCNS as member) and Rear Admiral Harinder Singh was unanimously approved for promotion as Vice Admiral for his 'excellent track record' and was graded as 'first in the order of merit' amongst all the officers considered. To quote from the minutes of the Promotion Board meeting "Rear Admiral Harinder Singh (Sl. No.1). The Board found this candidate to be consistently outstanding officer with excellent track record. He had held wide ranging operational, administrative, command and staff assignments and had commanded the Eastern Fleet with distinction. In inter se numerical grading, he ranked first in order of merit amongst all the officers in this consideration list. The Board found this officer eminently suitable for promotion to the rank of Vice Admiral and accordingly graded him 'B'."

ii)   February 1997 - Application submitted to go

abroad (three months in advance of travel). Naval Headquarters approved the application.

iii) May 1997 - Visited Russia with family (private visit). Stayed with Commodore (retired) Chowdhary at Moscow who is a family friend since school days. Course-mate at NDA (1958 onwards) and thereafter worked together in Navy.

iv) Naval Attaché, Moscow was also kept fully informed of places of stay, etc.

v) Subsequently, when Chief of Naval Staff charged him - through an entry in the ACR ten months later - with availing of lavish hospitality, the above facts were pointed out in the ROG submitted by Vice Admiral Harinder Singh. It was also mentioned in the ROG that incidentally, several other senior naval officers had also availed of Commodore Chowdhary's hospitality. None of this could be contradicted by the Chief of Naval Staff.

vi) June 97 – On return from leave, Vice Admiral Harinder Singh called on Admiral Bhagwat and discussed his visit also. No objections or questions were raised by Naval Headquarters or by his immediate superior authority from May 1997 till March 1998.

vii) November 1997 - Chief of Naval Staff wrote confidential report of Vice Admiral Harinder Singh. No adverse comments about having availed of hospitality, interest in shares, etc. were communicated to Vice Admiral Harinder Singh.

viii) 18th December 1997 - Vice Admiral Harinder Singh wrote to Chief of Naval Staff apprehending denial of posting as PSO in view of his past animosity connecting with the processing of adverse inputs/reports against the then Captain

Vishnu Bhagwat and again when the then Rear Admiral Harinder Singh was posted in Naval Headquarters Assistant Chief of Personnel. This apprehension was also based on informally announced decision of Chief of Naval Staff within the Naval hierarchy to bypass Vice Admiral Harinder Singh and Rear Admiral Raman Puri in the appointment of PSOs.

ix)   28th February 1998 - First vacancy of PSO arose on retirement of Vice Admiral P.S. Das. The Chief of Naval Staff not only did not seek ACC approval appointment of a PSO beforehand but did not submit any proposal for ACC approval till 23rd April 1998. In the meantime, w.e.f. 01 Mar 98, he appointed Rear Admiral M.J. Singh, who was lower in seniority as Deputy Chief of Naval Staff without approval even of Ministry of Defence not to talk of ACC bypassing two officer senior to him namely Vice Admiral Harinder Singh and Rear Admiral R. Puri, thus confirming the apprehensions expressed as mentioned above.

x)   18th March 1998- On the ACR recorded by Vice Admiral P.S. Das (outstanding entries given in all respects), Vishnu Bhagwat as Chief of Naval Staff and Reviewing Officer recorded his adverse comments on the hospitality, interest in shares and absence of the officer during Operation Leech, thus clearly confirming the apprehensions of Vice Admiral Harinder Singh already expressed in December 1997.

xi)   23rd March 1998 - Vice Admiral Harinder Singh submitted his ROG charging Chief of Naval Staff with favouritism in the matter of personnel appointments in Navy, of past animosity and being guided by his wife. In this, he also made passing references, which were interpreted as having communal overtones.

xii) 13th April 1998 - Vice Admiral Harinder Singh submitted his second ROG seeking expunction of adverse remarks and appointment as PSO (not as Deputy Chief of Naval Staff but any PSO level post or equivalent).

xiii) 23rd April 1998 - Naval Headquarters sent the proposal for appointment of PSO's in violation of seniority bypassing - Vice Admiral Harinder Singh and Raman Puri.

xiv) 30th April 1998 - Naval Headquarters issued show cause notice to Vice Admiral Harinder Singh making allegations against Chief of Naval Staff.

xv) 22nd May 1998 - Vice Admiral Harinder Singh wrote to Ministry of Defence for redressal of his grievances because Naval Headquarters had not disposed off his ROG within the 30-day period stipulated in the Navy Regulations. Raksha Mantri intervened at this stage and passed orders to this effect on file.

xvi) 4th June 1998 - Ministry of Defence, with the approval of the Raksha Mantri wrote to Naval Headquarters requesting reconsideration of proposal. Ministry of Defence did not indicate any preference for appointing any particular officer to any particular post of PSO. It merely asked the Chief of Naval Staff to reconsider the proposal giving regard to the principle of seniority as otherwise resentment and frustration were likely.

xvii) 5th June 1998 - Finding that his ROGs were not being disposed of, (neither accepted nor rejected) Vice Admiral Harinder Singh filed a Writ Petition in Calcutta High Court against the Show Cause Notice.

xviii) 8th June 1998 – Naval Headquarters replied to Ministry of Defence letter dated 4th June 1998 questioning the "knowledge, control or jurisdiction" of the government, thus effectively refusing to reconsider their proposal.

xix) 23rd June 1998 - Calcutta High Court passed orders that Ministry of Defence alone should deal with the matter and made adverse references against Chief of Naval Staff "for having dealt with this matter in the first place".

xx) 7th July 1998 - Ministry of Defence wrote to Chief of Naval Staff in reply to their letter dated 8th June 1998 pointing out the correct position both in respect of principle of seniority and the concept of Cabinet control.

xxi) 13th July 1998 - Naval Headquarters reply again finding fault with the government letter dated 7th July 1998.

xxii) 12th August 1998 – Adverse entries in the ACR if Vice Admiral Harinder Singh expunged by Ministry of Defence.

On analysis of the adverse remarks given by the ex-CNS and the various documents which were examined in the Ministry, it was found that the then FOC-in-C Eastern Naval Command, who was the Commanding Officer of Vice Admiral Harinder Singh had written a letter which stated that the Naval Headquarters had given the responsibility of conducting Operation Leech-II to him and that he at no point of time had considered it necessary to recall Vice Admiral Harinder Singh from leave. Nor had anyone from Naval Headquarters suggested to him that this be done. He even stated that it was inconceivable that The Naval Headquarters would not have taken this step if this had been considered even remotely necessary. Similarly, about the officer's interest in shares, the Chief of Naval Staff has just referred to 'a reputation' without giving details or instances. On the other hand, it was found that the officer had been consistently given a very high grading in terms of integrity in his more than 30 years of service and according to the annual terms filed by him as required under Service Regulations, the officer himself had entered into no share transactions in the year 1995-96 and 1996-97. Similarly, in 1997-98, he had transacted only one item of share.

Regarding his stay at Moscow and at St. Petersburg on vacation, it was found that:

(a) The officer had taken prior approval for his visit. It was found that:

(b) In Moscow the officer and his wife stayed with Retired Commodore V.K. Chaudhary.

(c) The Vice Admiral is not dealing with procurement in his official duties and ex-Commodore Chaudhary is not dealing with any procurement by Indian Navy and there is nothing on record against him. Commodore Chaudhary and the officer have been childhood friends, have been brought up together and are course-mates since January 1959. Commodore Chaudhary and his family have visited the Vice Admiral in Port Blair and the whole Navy and the Chief of Naval staff are personally fully aware of their close friendship for 40 years.

(d) The officer had added that every single officer who has gone to Russia in the recent past has taken the hospitality of Commodore Chaudhary because of his similarity in ages, etc. without any adverse inferences being drawn.

All this makes for interesting reading and the judgment of the court is appended for readers to appreciate what the High Court in Calcutta thought of the matter.

President

The Hon'ble justice
Vinod Kumar Gupta

And

The Hon'ble Justice
Sujit Barman Roy.

November 5, 1998

DICTATED ORDER

THE COURT: The petitioner in this contempt application Admiral Vishnu Bhagwat is the serving Chief of Naval Staff. The respondent No.1 Vice Admiral Harinder Singh is one o his subordinates serving as Forress Commander fo Indian Navy. The respondent No.2 even though named individually as Mr. Ajit Kumar is the Defence Secretary in the Government of India but implemented in his official capacity and the respondent No.3, again Mr Ajit Kumar individually, has been impleaded in his present capacity. The respondent No.1 Mr. R.P.Bagai is the Joint Secretary (Navy) in the Defence Ministry, Government of India.

It appears that the respondent No.1 was aggrieved of a show cause notice dated 30th April 1998 issued by and at the instance of the petitioner , accordingly, he approached this Court by a writ application under Article 226 of the Constitution of India. On 15th June 1998 the learned Singhle Judge whom the writ application came, while issuing a or show cause in the writ application to the respondents therein, granted an interim order to the effect that the writ petitioner (respondent No.1)herein may file his reply to the show cause notice within a fortnight from date but that no further stops shall be taken by the authorities pursuant thereto without leave of the Court. The operative part of the order reads thus :-

"Till 6.7.98 there will be an interim order to the effect that without prejudice to the rights and contentions of the petitioner he would submit his reply to the show cause notice dated 30.4.98 issued by the Chief of Naval Staff within a fortnight from date but no further stops shall be taken by the respondent in pursuant thereto without the leave of Court".

The writ petitioner(respondent No.1 herein)did not feel satisfied with the aforesaid order passed by the learned Single Judge in his writ application and, accordingly, preferred an appeal under the Latters Patent which was disposed of by a Division Bench of this Court on23 rd June 1998. In this judgement the Division Bench recorded the statements made on behalf of the learned Advocates appearing respectively for this Central Government and the petitioner herein to the effect that the proceedings arising out of the show cause notice dated 30th April 1998 would be dealt with by the Ministry of Defence, Central Government, directly uninfluenced by the petitioner herein . Certain observations were made in the course of the judgement with regard to the allegations of malafide levelled by the writ petitioner. While disposing of the appeal, as far as the submission of to the show cause notice was concerned, the Division Bench observes that the writ petitioner was permitted, is he so wished, to file , reply directly to the Central Government. In fact the Divisional Bench judgement while dealing with issued by the learned Single Judge, it was observed that the learnt Singe Judge in the order under appeal had also permitted the appellant to submit his reply to the impugned show cause notice. It appears that as a a sequel to the aforesaid, a communication was issued on 12th August 1998 signed by the respondent No.4 and addressed to the respondent No.1 wherein the respondent No.1 was called upon to furnish his reply to the aforesaid show cause notice urgently. This is the part No.1 of the present contempt application filed by the petitioner. In this first part, the petitioner says that by not submitting his reply to the show cause notice within 15 days, as directed by the learned Singe Judge vide order dated 15th June 1998 and as reiterated by the Division Bench on 23 June 98 the respondent No.1 has committed contempt of this Court and that by asking him to submit his 2,3, and 4 have also committed contempt of this Court. That is the only allegation in so far as part No.1 is concerned.

The second part of the contempt application arises out of and relates to the passing of the order dated 6th October 1998 by the Central Government under the signatures of respondent No.4.

The order reads thus :-

"The Central Government has received by the reply dated 17.8.1998 to the show cause notice dated 10.4.1998 issued by NHO from Vice Admiral Harinder Singh.

Keeping in view the directions of the Calcutta High Court dated 23.6.1998 the Central Government has examined the reply to the show cause notice furnished by the Officer. After careful consideration of the relevant records, the reply furnished by the Officer and the unqualified apology tendered by him. The in which the Officer was placed and his past record, the Government has decided not to proceed further with the matter and the case is hereby closed.

Sd/-(R.P. Bagai)
Joint Secretary to the Government of India

It is the case of the petitioner in the second part that the Central Government by passing the aforesaid Order and while granting relief to respondent No.1 has acted illegally, contrary to the provisions of law relating to Navy and by violating all norms and Court orders has abused the judicial process. According to the petitioner, the passing of this order amounts to committing contempt of this Court. Since according to the petitioner, this Court had directed that the Central Government may dispose of the matter in accordance with law, by passing the aforesaid order illegally, the respondents have committed contempt of this court.

We were taken through certain averments contained in the Contempt application particularly in paras 14,15 and 16. Very grave and serious allegations, but unsubstantiated have been levelled by the petitioner against the respondents. What would be the consequence of levelling such allegations is not for us to consider or decide because these are neither pertinent nor relevant to the issue involved herein.

We, however clearly are of the view that in respect of neither part 1 nor part 2 has any contempt been committed by the respondents before us or any one of them. IN so far as part 1 is concerned, both the learned Single Judge and the Division Bench had merely permitted the writ petitioner (respondent No.1 herein) to submit his reply to the show cause notice, if he so wished. It was, therefore the absolute choice of the writ petitioner either to submit a reply or not to submit any reply and thus face consequences. The directions and observations contained in the orders of both the learned Single Judge and the Division Bench cannot by any stretch of imagination be construed to amount to him to submit his reply to the Show Cause notice. We reiterate that it was left open to the writ petitioner to do so if he so wished. Thus, whether the reply was submitted in2 weeks after 15th

June 1998 or two months or was not submitted at all, was for the writ petitioner to consider. This is one aspect of the matter. The other more important aspect is that the Central Government to whom the reply was to be submitted was not at all prevented by any order of this court from extending the period during which the reply was to be received. It was entirely for the Central Government to decide as to when should it receive the reply from the writ petitioner, if at all. Such action on the part of the Central Government, therefore, cannot at all be called amounting to committing contempt of this court because the Central Government or for that matter the respondent No.2 to 4 by asking the writ petitioner to submit the reply vide communication dated 12th August 1990 did not violate or disobey any order passed by this court.

In so far as the second part of the contempt application is concerned, despite great persuasion to ourselves we have failed to comprehend as to who even in anyone's wildest imagination can the passing of the order dated 6th October 1998 by the Central Govt. amount to committing contempt of this Court. By granting redressal to the writ petitioner, the Central Government has disposed of the proceedings. This Court did not at all indicate in any of its orders as to the manner in which the proceedings were to be disposed of nor did this court indicate as to what the result of such disposal ought to have been. In fact, very plainly speaking we fail to understand as to how can the petitioner feel himself aggrieved of the passing of the order dated 6th October 1998. This order does not adversely affect the petitioner in any manner nor does it cause any prejudice to him. The order dated 6th October 1998 is a matter directly between the Central Government and Respondent No.1. A related aspect cold be as to whether it is open for the petitioner to assail or challenge an order passed by the Central Government. We however refrain from making any comment on this issue.

From what we have observed, we have no manner of doubt that this Contempt Application is wholly misconceived and totally devoid of any merit. It is accordingly dismissed in limine.

The department is directed to supply certified xerox copies of this dictated order expeditiously.

OF WOMEN, WIVES IN THE SERVICES AND MRS NILOUFER BHAGWAT AND MRS. JAYA JAITLEY

'Behind every successful man there is a woman' is a well repeated cliché. The key word is behind him, and when she precedes him there is bound to befall some trouble. In the defence forces wives play a prominent role especially as an officer progresses in his service career. In India, where women have held subservient positions for long, the scene is changing for women. In the Armed Forces wives are married to men who are dealing with demanding roles at sea, in remote border areas and risk adventures in the air. It is but natural the service wife be it of a lowly sailor or the senior captain lives through constant fear of his life for the job entails challenging demands, and also have to suffer long periods of separation. In the Indian Navy Officers and men manning new ships and submarines were deputed to USSR in the 70s and were separated from their wives and families for over 13 months at a stretch. The psychological effects were traumatic. The bachelors did let their hair down with willing damsels behind the iron curtain, while the married ones moped and ached for their loved ones, but demands of a professional service career over ruled their lives.

While the dedicated soldier, sailor and airman serves his country away from house and hearth his wife does her bit to be his long distance anchor ashore, to care for his children, bring them up, collect the rations, pay the bills and struggle for a daily existence. Many women adapt to the big metropolises that the Navy habits, but others suffer in villages uneducated and often disjointed with their men. But they still hold their head high for the service her husband serves and so the wife is an important cog in the life of a serving man and in the social system of the Armed Forces. In the case of senior officers wives have to look after the welfare projects that the services have put into motion and arrange activities get-togethers to get the feel and mood of their units . In the Navy, barrakhanas, picnics, families day at sea, Diwali and other melas and welfare activities by the Naval Wives Welfare Association are part of daily life. But another aspect is that wives also unwittingly get involved in pushing the progress of their husbands service career. There is nothing wrong in it, if is done in a dignified manner with service interest at heart. A senior service wife should never be over demanding, bossing or be seen to be meddling in the service aspect of a ship, an establishment, station, a command or the service as a whole. Today many wives have also taken up professional jobs and have to balance their husbands needs to be involved in service functions, and yet do justice to their own demanding tasks at work. It is very challenging and makes married life full of dynamics of pulls and pushes from all sides. In the present case Admiral Vishnu Bhagwat's wife Niloufer was a fire brand advocate who was baptized as a young lawyer as a junior to Mr. Rajni Patel in Mumbai. He was a renowned criminal lawyer and his reputation as a politician also, is still well remembered. Mrs. Bhagwat therefore always stood up for causes, stormed the lower and high courts of Bombay and had built up a reputation as a lawyer with tenacity. The judges knew her. This could have been her asset. But when she saw her husband being sidelined for the Fleet Commander's post, which she believed Vishnu deserved, she chose the high legal turf to fight the battle and trap the senior officers of the Indian Navy. The result was the 400 page writ petition which came as a bombshell and something novel for the Indian Navy. A service that thrived on professionalism, technology, camaraderie and dedication was now dealing with 400 pages of allegations, some so dangerous and slanderous that the CNS Nadkarni called for a 'courts martial' of the petitioner, and this has been highlighted in a full chapter with verse and quote.

Mrs. Bhagwat took on the role of Vishnu's lawyer, more than a service wife. She began to look at acts and omissions in the Indian Navy which are bound to crop up with a legal twist and blew them out of proportion and used legalese to make them sound as illegal acts. The average officer and sailor did not know the details, but it had mesmerized the higher echelon of the Navy and appears to be the beginning of a sinister plot. Mrs. Bhagwat also took on the case of another senior officer's son-in-law's marital case. It sullied the atmosphere The matter took nasty turns and the case finally was resolved in the supreme court. Today I understand fully why that senior

officer as Vice Chief of the Naval Staff did not wish
to serve a day under Admiral Vishnu Bhagwat.

In the case of Bhagwat's dismissal Mrs. Bhagwat
became his defendant, spokeswoman and lawyer and
went on the TV brazenly with aggressive postures to
defend her client and husband. For the first two
weeks Bhagwat observed silence on his dismissal . A
service already shocked by removal of a Chief, and a
nation not used to seeing a service wife so vociferous
and shrill, and that too of a service chief in the role
she played, did not take it well. Mrs. Bhagwat also
vitiated the atmosphere and hurled charges and
accusations against the Akali Dal , George Fernandes
and one of them were against Shrimati Jaya Jaitley, the
Secretary of the Samata party. Mrs. Jetley ex Jay
Chettur from Kerala and did her college education in
Mirada College in New Delhi. She is the wife of a
senior IAS officer and friends who knew her in
college rate her an above average and talented
personality. On TV she comes off as a very articulate
person. More she came in to prominence as being as
being close to George Fernandes of the Samata party.
In an exchange of letters in the Hindustan Times Jaya
Jaitley pulled up the editor for quoting the remarks
made by Niloufer Bhagwat about her and one would
have thought the matter would have died a natural
death as Mrs. Bhagwat was not seen or heard of in the
media once Vishnu began defending his case in the
media. It was not to be.

Jaya Jaitley came out with a piece on Niloufer
Bhagwat in the Pioneer titled "Wife, Lawyer,
Politician or Mouthpiece". Excerpts are reproduced
as this piece and another on 7 April by her titled "
The Congress's Hall of Integrity " in connection with

the Bhagwat drama depict the involvement of the two women who did not see eye to eye when Bhagwat was the Chief and had many social interactions with his Minister of Defence George Fernandes."

An editorial in one of the national dailies felt the need to commend the former Chief of Navy Staff for exercising graceful restraint after his sacking. This demonstrates the extent to which both the Press and commentators who claim to be political or defence analysts have decided to wear blinkers and pursue their private agendas. While everyone reads interviews conducted by the media with Ms. Niloufer Bhagwat with amusement, disbelief or consternation, no one has had the courage to say "Look, the Emperor has no clothes" Admiral Vishnu Bhagwat can by no means claim credit for being gracefully restrained when he allows his wife to run riot in the official residential premises of the CNS and to throw wild accusations at everybody. Ms Bhagwat presumes that her legal expertise can carry her through as she accuses political parties of hidden agendas, various ministers of being co-conspirators, I.K. Gujral and son of being connected with arms dealers. However, the very nature and range of her remarks raises serious questions about how the Admiral can acquiesce by being a silent spectator, while Ms. Bhagwat blatantly slips from the role of wife to lawyer to politician to slander monger. Ms. Bhagwat began her diatribe immediately after the Admiral's dismissal by raising the banner of a saffron plot because of her participation in the inquiry conducted by the Sri Krishna Commission into the riots in Mumbai. However, no one asked whether it was she who was dismissed that she should put the focus on herself.

She drew all the attention as Bhagwat's wife and referred to Vice Admiral Harinder Singh's remark of her being half-Muslim as communal (which it was). However, her claim to speak at all has been as Bhagwat's lawyer in the Harinder case. She extends her fear of communalism in other interviews where she says that Vice Admiral Harinder Singh's and the Akali Dal's communal interests would now spread from the Navy to the Army. This kind of threat or fear has no place in the brief of a mere lawyer. The anti-secular bogey was quickly deflated when it was discovered that the new CNS Admiral Sushil Kumar was, by sheer chance, a Christian. Except for one reporter who crudely asked the new CNS why he had shed the surname Isaac, everyone including Ms. Bhagwat let it drop quietly. Next came the arms dealers angel. Now what would a lawyer, whose brief it is to deal with a case against a client on a matter of promotions, be doing flinging mud on the entire Navy by telling the Sunday magazine (January 10-17, 1999), that all Naval appointments were bought and sold" Does a lawyer whose client is the Chief of Naval Staff, have regular information about the entire Navy's fraudulent appointments from well before the Harinder Singh case came up in the Calcutta High Court? Can the CNS give such wide-ranging information to his lawyer or was he sharing his knowledge/suspicions with the lawyer as his wife? It is the wife or the lawyer who knows that Admiral K.K. Kohli bought his appointment or is it permissible for the wife persona to share information received in the bedroom or on the naval cocktail party gossip circuit with the lawyer persona who can then use this to elaborate accusations on behalf of her client, a.k.a. her husband? In an interview to the Hindustan Times on January 10, 1999 when asked to substantiate her allegation that the Defence Minister was planting stories in newspapers, Ms. Bhagwat called him "temperamentally low" because he was one of those associated with "the very people (she presumably means Lok Nayak Jayaprakash Narayan) in asking the armed forces to revolt" and because he supposedly "went around attempting to blow up institutions:" (she mistakes railway tracks for institutions). Both issues demonstrate a warped understanding of those political times. JP led the fight of the Opposition against the widespread corruption of the Congress and subsequently the Emergency which shackled democracy. Mr. George Fernandes led the underground battle against Indira Gandhi's dictatorship and declared that any means were legitimate to fight an illegitimate Government. Jayaprakash Narayan has recently been awarded the Bharat Ratna and Mr. Fernandes has held prominent positions in all non-Congress governments. Is it her case (not legal so it must be political) that all non-Congress prime ministers are poor judges of character? In another interview she describes her husband's sacking as worse than the Emergency. By comparing Bhagwat's removal with the throttling of democracy, along with all the horrors that went with it such as the jailing of Opposition leaders, changing the constitution unconstitutionally, censoring the Press and suspending civil laws she is attempting to paint her husband's fate as being of greater importance than the fate of democracy in India. Did the emergence of Ms. Bhagwat the politician resurface here because the "secular" angle did not fructify?

Ranjit B. Rai, R.P. Singh

Such remarks about one of the darkest periods in free India's history can only be a political or personal opinion as no wife is permitted formally to fight her husband's professional battles and no lawyer can throw her own political preferences into a client's brief.

The deliberate misuse of her position as Vishnu Bhagwat's lawyer to personally attack individuals on his dismissal, for which he himself has chosen not to go to Court, is being allowed to pass unnoticed. Slander against Mr. Gujral and his son, Admiral Kohli for buying his job, the Appointments Committee of Cabinet for the political-criminal nexus and Jaya Jaitley for being asocial climber ad worse, could only be the voice of a wife since responsible lawyers and politicians seldom stoop so low or risk making such accusations. This political persona of Ms. Bhjagwat further flowers in her interview to the Sunday when she speaks of the hidden agenda of the Akali Dal. Suddenly she deduced that the purpsoe of Mr. Fernandes being given the task of heading the Committee to sort out the Udhamsingh Nagar problem was actually only one layer of the agenda. Her political eye(couldn't be wifely or legal)spotted the hidden agenda of the Akalis in this Committee which was to induct people of their choice into senior positions in the Services and Vice Admiral Harinder Singh was one such candidate. Yet in the Hindustan Times interview when asked how she knows so much about the Navy, she says, "If you ask me anything about the Navy not related to the case, I wouldn't know". The wife knew that all appointments in the Navy are bought and sold, the lawyer knows Harinder is a Sikh who doesn't deserve a certain job because he

96

criticised her as a wife, and the politician spotted a hidden agenda in the Udhamsingh Nagar Committee which no other seasoned or unseasoned politician in the country could do. Which is the real Niloufer Bhagwat? Wife, lawyer or politician? Or is to be accepted that she can merge all three voices while Vishnu Bhagwat stands approvingly by her side ? The most dangerous political persona she has revealed yet appeared in the Times of India interview of January 18, 1999 conducted in Mumbai. On being asked whether the Directorate of Naval Intelligence flouted protocol by protesting directly to the Pakistani High Commission about a Pakistani aircraft trailing an Indian Naval ship on June 12, 1998, she answers: "The Admiral had informed the External Affairs Ministry about the incident with the copy marked to the Defence Ministry. When the Pakistani High commission protested, the Indian Government endorsed its stand. I wonder if there is a nexus between the Indian Government and the Pakistani High Commission. Why should the Government support the Pakistani High commission when there is an undeclared war in Kashmir?". In effect, she accuses the MEA, i.e. the Government of India, of treason., Even Mr. Bal Thackeray has not gone that far. Yet Vishnu Bhagwat is described as remaining gracefully silent while she as a person in her own right flowers in the avatar of a loose cannon to serve as his mouthpiece.

Jaya Jaitley also got upset when the Congress party took up Bhagwat's case to ask for a Joint Parliamentary Committee and spewed her venom on the Congress party leader Mrs. Sonia Gandhi, listed. Charges against Bhagwat and questioned the integrity of Lieutenant General P.N. Hoon who had filed a PIL in Mumbai. He has threatened to sue Mrs. Jaya Jaitley for her article in the Pioneer on April 7, 99. Some excerpts indicate how much Jaya was concerned about the Bhagwat case.

Quote

Apart from the fact that Admiral Vishnu Bhagwat's affidavits consist of wild innuendoes, and irresponsible allegations without any evidence to back his words, it is indeed alarming that accusations of a dismissed man full of anger, humiliation and revenge should be made a political weapon, quite neglecting the danger to national security interests, the morale of the services and the delicate relationship between civil and military authority. Many countries in the past have dismissed service chiefs.

General Douglas MacArthur of the United States is a famous example, and Pakistan's Chief of Army Staff, General Jahangir Karamat, who was eased out by being made to resign, the most recent one, but neither did they start throwing mud at everyone around them, nor did they run for help to the nearest opposition party. The utter recklessness of such action is only matched by the Congress party president who gives an integrity certificate to a person found (a) tampering with the ACRs of officers; (b) lying about being raided by the Central Bureau of Investigation (CBI) and Intelligence Bureau (IB); (c) lying about not having received representations from senior officers; (d) refusing to provide files to the highest civilian authority; (e) leaking highly classified information: (f) "listing" non-existent phone calls made between the Defence Secretary and his immediate junior (g) sending, against all diplomatic norms, a letter of protest directly to the Pakistan Embassy about violation of territory of a Pakistani ship (The Union Government had to face the embarrassment of having this letter sent back to it by the Pakistan Embassy.); (h) carrying his wife as the "lawyer of the Chief of Naval Staff" in a navy aircraft without her being authorised as such, to file a contempt petition against his own Ministry; (i)demeaning the highest civilian position in the Ministry of Defence by accusing the Defence Minister of aiding terrorists and gun-runners and even harbouring them in his house.

Unquote

The moral of the story is that service / professional matters should be left outside the bedroom and wives should continue to stand behind their husbands for the latter to progress. When wives try to stand beside, or in front of, their husbands, their husband's judgement could be coloured and they may well have to side step to let others pass.

THE LEGAL ASPECTS OF THE DISMISSAL OF THE CHIEF OF THE NAVAL STAFF VISHNU BHAGAWAT

Wednesday 30 December 1998 will go down as a low water mark in the history of the Indian Navy. On that day the incumbent Navy Chief Admiral Vishnu Bhagwat was unceremoniously relieved of his job by the President of India under powers vested in him as Commander in Chief of the Armed Forces . In terms of Article 53 of the Constitution Part V titled THE UNION all executive powers of the Union are vested in the President and he is to exercise these himself or through officers subordinate to him but in accordance with the provisions of the Constitution . The section carries on to say

(2) ." Without prejudice to the generality of the foregoing provision, the supreme command of the Defence Forces of the Union shall be vested in the President and the exercise thereof shall be regulated by law."

To comply with the directive of Article 52(2), separate laws for the services were inked and these were based on the British patterns . The Army , Navy and Air Force Acts came into force in 1957 and have governed the disciplinary aspects of the three services and are still in force and interpreted by the Judge Advocate of the three services and the judiciary. There are differences between the legal provisions of the three services and the Court Martial procedures are completely at variance . In the Navy Act it is specified that the President of India is the competent authority to Court Martial the Chief of the Naval Staff . This route was however not taken to bring Bhagwat to book .

Bhagwat's dismissal has been processed under the provisions of Article 310 of the Constitution and Section 15 of the Navy Act . Defence service officers serve at the pleasure of the President, who can withdraw this pleasure on the advice of the Council of Ministers vide article 74 of the Constitution . It goes on to say :-

74(2) "The question whether any, and if so what, advice was tendered by the Ministers to the President shall not be inquired into in any court ."

In the recent Bhagwat case it has come to light from statements by concerned parties that at some stage the communications between the Defence Secretary and the CNS had broken down and those between CNS and Defence Minister came under strain. This was exacerbated by the CNS Bhagwat refusing to accept the Appointments Committee decision to appoint Vice Admiral Harinder Singh the seventh senior most officer in the Navy ,as the Deputy Chief of the Naval Staff. Bhagwat took refuge in the semantics of the Article 184 in the Regulations that stipulates that all appointments above the rank of Captain shall be made by the Government on the recommendations of the CNS. However in civilian control the Cabinet is superior and legal experts suggest their final decision can overrule a recommendation. Earlier Harinder Singh it appears had been given an adverse report by Bhagwat and so the officer had represented. This was rejected by the Navy so he would have made what is called a Statutory Complaint to the Government . The Regulations Navy permits that if the aggrieved person is not satisfied by the Government reply or no reply is received in three months he is free to appeal to the High Court for redress and this is what Vice Admiral Harinder Singh did in the Calcutta High Court under Article 226 of the Constitution . Bhagwat as a Rear Admiral had followed the same route in 1990 and filed a 400 page writ petition in the Bombay High Court when he was being denied command of Western Fleet.

The allegations in the voluminous writ No 2757 of 1990 has allegations against many . Shri George Fernandes referred to this affidavit made under oath in some detail in a television interview and in the media . Hence a brief explanation is in order . The writ included allegations that Vice Admiral S K Jain , Bhagwat's immediate superior and the Chief of Naval Staff Admiral J G Nadkarni had tampered with his report to deny him the Fleet Command and that US trained officers and those with children in USA were CIA agents. There were allegations of corruption , breaches of budget spending and custom regulations and derogatory remarks on abilities of officers and high Government officials. This paralyzed the Navy.

If the Navy had to institute inquiries in to these wide ranging allegations, many would not have held water. However it would have taken months and years to follow the Naval regulations of Inquiries and the Navy's senior officers would have been employed in the task till they retired. Some compromise on Bhagwat's confidential reports it is reported and he was given command of the Eastern Fleet . Fleet command is a brownie point to be considered for FOC-in-C of the operational Western and Eastern Commands and then for CNS. Bhagwat withdrew his petition . Not much is known of what happened to the matter in the Ministry of Defence and the Defence Minister George Fernandes is the first Minister to have raised it in the defence of his bold action along with other misdemeanors of Bhagwat . He has also stated Bhagwat was almost Court Martialed in 1991. A journalist Ketan Modi has this to say in a leading newspaper on 21 April 1991.

"Strangely , the division bench of the High Court permitted withdrawal of the writ even though only one of the 12 respondents –The Union of India was served with a notice of motion . Even Jain krew nothing of it . "

In the aftermath Vice Admiral S K Jain was superseded by Vice Admiral L Ramdas who become the 15th Chief of the Naval Staff in 1991 in a high voltage drama. In September 1996 Bhagwat took over as the 17th Chief of Naval Staff from Admiral VPS Shekhawat. This is the background and someday historians will unearth the details .

Events moved swiftly on 30 December 1998. Bhagwat attended a lecture at the USI that morning . RM George Fernandes summoned Vice Admiral Sushil Kumar FO C in C Southern Command in Kochi to Delhi and he arrived in secrecy in an ARC plane controlled by RAW. He met the RM and was escorted to the famous White Office in South Block . By 5.30 pm for the first time a serving Chief was dismissed unceremoniously and Admiral Sushil Kumar nee Issacs took over as CNS. In Pakistan the Navy Chief and the Army Chief have resigned at their leaders behest when they were told their time was up. The Government and the media labeled it as " CNS sacked " which is correct in civil parlance, but not in the Armed Forces .. An Armed Force lives and breathes on pride called Izzat. He is not to be humiliated unless he is guilty of negligence ,cowardice , corruption , anti-national acts or gone beserk for which the court martial route is open . Admiral R H Tahiliani ex CNS and S C Chopra ex VCNS both had faced court martials as Captains for endangering their ships INS Vikrant and Betwa but were honourably acquitted by their peers . In those days a court martial was mandated.

Mr George Fernandes in all his wisdom did not wish to follow the court martial route and so went the Cabinet decision route via Article 310 of the Constitution . Now no questions can be asked . He could have executed the deed with civility for he was not dealing with a railway trade union , Coca Cola multinational company or Nestles . It is left to the Government's discretion to allow pension and other benefits or even to deny them in such cases .

The drama will not affect the fine Indian Navy except its morale will certainly sag for a while and if Bhagwat has been brash, as it comes out , the next Chief can easily get the naval ship back to even keel . But if someone has tarnished the communal image of the Indian Navy and he or she gets away without recrimination then it will be a sad commentary for the country's leaders and the learned cabinet that took this bold decision . Also the Defence Ministry system of keeping Service HQs out of decision making needs urgent rectification and there is a crying need for a Chief of Defence Staff to cohese the three services for operations , planning and intelligence. He will also be the senior professional adviser to the Defence Minister. The three Chiefs system is not working because the Defence Secretary is doing this job , for which he is ill qualified as has come out in this case .

THE REVERBERATIONS OF WRIT PETITION OF THEN REAR ADMIRAL VISHNU BHAGWAT NO. 2757 OF 1990 FILED IN THE BOMBAY HIGH COURT BY MRS. BHAGWAT

The episode a la Bhagwat and his removal from office and the associated washing of dirty linen in public can never be fully appreciated or the canvas of the times since late 1980s, in the Indian Navy, be colourfully illustrated for the reader, unless the matter of the Writ petition No.2757 by then Rear Admiral Vishnu Bhagwat filed in the Bombay High Court on 12th September 1990 and later withdrawn, is made public and analysed dispassionately. The 404-page Writ petition which included copious, personal and confidential correspondence exchanged in the Navy, enclosures from magazines, extracts of regulations and severe charges and innuendoes of wrongdoing against various officers and authorities surprised the 15 respondents and the many concerned parties which were not respondents, but were mentioned either by name or insinuation and with specific acts of omissions and commissions with dates and details. The petition was filed against the Chief of Naval Staff

Admiral J.G. Nadkarni and included the Flag Officer Commanding-in-Chief Western Naval Command Vice Admiral S. Jain, who was Bhagwat's immediate boss, the Chief of Personnel Vice Admiral V.L. Koppikar who controlled appointments in New Delhi and all the five Executive branch Rear Admirals immediately junior to Bhagwat, P.S. Das, Kailash Kohli, V.K. Malhotra, Peter Debrass and Avnish Tandon and Peter De'Brass and the Defence Minister who was also the Prime Minister Shri V.P. Singh and the Union of India and others. The Writ petition contained a lot of material, that in normal course would hardly be available to a serving naval personnel.

If someone in the Indian Navy had brought a small or mini item from abroad in a ship it was there in the Writ in print. If someone had received a poor or good Annual Confidential report it was there and it was explained how he got it. The supposed marking system of Annual Confidential Reports was touched upon and Bhagwat stated on oath that he had assisted the CNS as his Naval Assistant to draw up a template of all officers up to then Captain Madhavendra Singh and inked their prospective appointments, as perspective planning for the next decade. Bhagwat's name as a prospective for Fleet Command was in the scheme of things. This was revealing and one day I jokingly told him that if he knew my days were numbered in the Navy he could have informed me, when we were together pulling the Navy's boat in NHQ and Op Pawan was in full swing. My wife would not have had to consult astrologers. The promotion statistics of all officers who have attended Naval War College at New Port Rhode Island, USA were tabulated in some detail to compare the Indian Naval scene. If someone had been friendly in the Indian Navy with someone else it was there. If an officer was related to the Defence Secretary it was highlighted, and if an officer's close relation had closed some deal in his capacity as an individual many moons ago it was all bared there. If someone had made excessive telephone calls the figures of the bills were indicated. The name of the Company that was supplying spares for HDW submarines and how the fifth and sixth HDW class submarines were to be financed was explained and the financial system in the Navy's Plans Directorate highlighted. How single-handedly Bhagwat contributed as a Commodore to get nuclear submarine INS Chakra on lease from Russia against opposition from respondents and how and why specifications of missile stowage temperatures were changed in the Navy, were tabled to the High Court in the Writ. USA's foreign policy was discussed and if any officer had his children studying or obtaining a green card in that scheming country, or an officer happened to do a course at the Naval War College he was branded suspect, and those that did so, were definitely involved in a conspiracy of sorts in the Indian Navy because they all got promoted and were all made Fleet Commanders. If an officer attended a diplomatic party it was there, along with the Government of India, conduct of rules duly highlighted which dissuades Government officials to drink at functions. If officers acquired flats in Bombay from a Cooperative Society the subject matter and how much it cost was discussed. If INS Andaman sank off the coast of Vishakapatnam it was included with blame portioned. The list can go on but the genuine grievance of Rear Admiral Vishnu Bhagwat was that he had been denied command of the Eastern Fleet in late 1989 and then the Western Fleet in 1990. Bhagwat claimed he had being superseded by Rear Admirals P.S. Das and Kailash Kohli respectively who were immediately junior to him. Bhagwat feared that even in the next round he may not find a berth as Fleet Commander and by end 1990 when a new Chief of Naval Staff was to be appointed on retirement of Nadkarni, a vacancy for a Vice-Admiral was likely, and he would be out of the reckoning. The tussle for the next Chief was between the senior-most Vice-Admirals S. Jain and L. Ramdas, the next in line, who were both experienced and able officers of the First Course of JSW and Jain had been given an extension to ensure he was in the running. In India there is no defined practice of selecting the Chief and finally Ramdas became CNS on 1 Dec 1990, and the press in articles insinuated that it was Bhagwat's Writ that tipped the balance in Ramdas's favour.

President R.V. Venkataraman in his book "My Presidential Years" has this to say on the subject. "The choice of the Chiefs of the Army, Navy and air Force is made by the Government after assessment of their service records by the Defence Minister and Prime Minister. Admiral Nadkarni Chief of Naval Staff was to retire on November 30, 1990. Earlier Nadkarni had extended the services of Vice-Admiral Jain who was retiring before CNS so that he would be eligible for consideration for the post of Admiral when time for choice came. This was nothing new. Similar action had been taken in case of Air Vice-Marshal Katre and Vice-Admiral Tahiliani. The natural expectation was that Vice Admiral Jain might be promoted as CNS over the next senior Vice-Admiral Ramdas."

"Prime Minister V.P. Singh had discussed the matter with me and said that he preferred Vice-Admiral Ramdas for the post of Chief. I had told V.P. Singh that I had no personal preferences and that he could communicate his proposal for my approval. On receipt of the file, I perused the records and approved it. After Chandrashekhar became Prime Minister, he asked me whether the appointment of Ramdas could be reconsidered. He also sent Defence Secretary Vohra to explain the reasons to me. I told the Defence Secretary that orders for appointment of Ramdas had already been issued and gazetted and any attempt to overturn the decision, except on very serious charges of fraud, misrepresentation or suppression of material facts, would seriously damage the morale of the services. I also expressed doubts whether an order already passed could be revoked. Vohra inquired if Nadkarni could be given an extension for one month and the matter reviewed. I replied that it would set bad precedent and every Chief of Staff would try to wangle an extension in future."

"I also felt that a Chief on extension would suffer a serious loss of prestige as the officers and men would look upon him as a lame duck chief. On November 27, two Cabinet ministers called on me and discussed this issue. I explained to them the need to maintain high standards of discipline in the armed forces and also the sanctity of a decision. I cautioned them that there would be public suspicion of political interference if the appointment was changed with a change in government."

On November 28, I hosted a dinner for the retiring Navy Chief. As usual I invited the CNS designate, all Chiefs of Staff and retired Chiefs resident in Delhi. When my staff asked whether there would be any embarrassment in inviting Ramdas, I said that as long as his appointment remained in force he was entitled to attend. Ramdas took over as Chief of Naval Staff on December 1, 1990 and except for stray references in the Press, the matter died out."

The Writ petition's contents were being quoted freely as all the respondents in the writ had been served the voluminous copies and photocopying machines were working overtime. Not being experts on Article 14 and 226 of the Constitution, the respondents were paralysed as to what they should do. About that time, INS Nilgiri visited Singapore in 1990 on a very successful Flag showing official visit, flying the Flag of the Fleet Commander, Eastern Fleet, my term-mate and friend, like Bhagwat, Admiral P.S. Das. I was exposed for the first time to snippets about this document, which had mesmerised the higher echelons of the Navy and worried junior ranks. The prelude to all this of course, was the redressal of grievance and statutory complaints tabled by Bhagwat to his superiors which had not satisfied him and he was convinced that there were sinister designs to pass him over.

From Singapore I decided to send some goodies like chocolates and soup packets for my son left behind in India, but the officers were reluctant to oblige, and I report this as someone who had served as long as Bhagwat had in the IN, and had not seen such pettiness in this great service. Journalists and some others who have perused the document have likened it to a novelette, because events and activities of daily unclassified and classified service life were made into plots and dramatically exaggerated into legalese. The contents of this document to a layman reveals it as more than a legal petition, but an excellent legal petition it was, because answers were not easy to come by on what Bhagwat's lawyer wife had committed on full scape legal paper. It did contain some of the minor and major infirmities of actions that go into the promotion system in a small but expanding service, where the Chief has all controlling power as the senior-most reviewing officer. But, in the Armed Forces, one has to have faith in the people one is led by, in the larger interests of the service. Bhagwat felt he was wronged, he had a valid case and he was not going to take it lying down. Hence, he left no stone unturned to level charges, which the Ministry of Defence also analysed in a document widely circulated in April 1999.

Before this landmark action, hardly any officer in the Indian Navy had gone to court, courting promotion, and almost no technical Flag officers attempted promotion by the court route. The maximum step taken by aggrieved officers after a letter of grievance was rejected by the Chief of Naval Staff was to tender a Statutory complaint to the Government as per the Regulations IN, and hope justice would be dispensed, if any wrong doing came to light. Earlier Chiefs of Naval Staff and Chiefs of Personnel also had the courage to call officers and explain why the particular individual did not merit promotion or get a particular appointment, but it appears this honourable practice was no longer followed. All senior promotion boards are headed by the CNS and Commanding-in-Chiefs are members. It is well understood that everyone cannot merit promotion in a steep pyramidical structure, and as emotional individuals that we Indians are, some subjectivity does creep in. In the Army an independent General has been appointed to review cases as an independent body in the Complaints and Advisory Board and offer impartial comments on cases of representation. The Navy has none and the Ministry has little expertise to oppose the Chief, though Defence Ministers like Mulayam Singh Yadav have imposed their nominees for promotion against the recommendations of the Service. If one failed to merit promotion because there was faith in the system that decided matters, then like a good soldier one faded away and tried one's hand in the civilian field or whatever, including re-employment which was offered selectively at mid-level ranks. Court cases were also seen as dilatory and expensive methods of redressal, which everyone could not afford. The government has conceded that it will establish a Service tribunal like the Civil Appellate Tribunal for civil officers. It must.

Therefore, the voluminous wide ranging Writ filed by Bhagwat was a new 'googly' in cricket parlance, and is the genesis of the tremendous upheavals and machinations, the Indian Navy experienced from 1990 to the time when Bhagwat was dismissed by the Minister of Defence, George Fernandes, whose own political career has been controversy ridden. He has relied heavily on the comments offered by the then Chief on the withdrawn Writ, which have been highlighted by MOD. The drama is still not over as the BJP coalition government, the one in power, that took the decision, has fallen. It was felled on the Bhagwat issue, which unfortunately has got politicised. It was Ms. Jayalalalitha who took the BJP to task and asked for Bhagwat's reinstatement, George Fernandes' neck and a JPC. Fernandes has often referred to this Writ petition and the correspondence connected with it. India Today has reproduced some startling notings by Admiral Nadkarni on Defence Ministry files on his recommendations on the petition calling for Bhagwat's dismissal or court martial. Promotion board notations and confidential reports of officers have also appeared in the media recently. Hence to view these without appreciating the contents of that petition is to be ill informed. It needs to be bared since the after effects will continue to reverberate in the Navy unless the matter is appreciated and the wounds, many systemic, healed. If this is not done, the ghost of that Writ will continue to haunt the present senior and mid-level generation of the fine Indian Navy, which as an institution has borne the storm well. It speaks volumes of its professionalism.

HISTORY

By 1988, as the Director of Naval Intelligence, I became a bystander as I was superseded and passed over for promotion and overtaken by two of my team-mates junior to me in the Navy List seniority since the 60s, namely Vishnu Bhagwat and P.S. Das both deservedly became Rear Admirals, and adorned two stars. Both officers had excellent track records and Das who had topped the course but had lost seniority enroute was the Director of Naval Plans and Bhagwat was just completing his term as the Naval Assistant to the Chief of Naval Staff Admiral, R.H. Tahiliani. We were all considered together for promotion and surprisingly bunched into a big batch, that of three NDA and direct entry courses, because the then CNS in 1987, Admiral R.H. Tahiliani, one of Navy's youngest Chiefs, and a very shrewd and able leader, decided to do some deep selection. He must have had his compulsions in the larger interests of an expanding Navy. He was also due to retire soon and young at 56 in 1987, yet an extension was not granted to him. Many now claim that he wanted to leave a mark on India's Navy and he made a template of all senior officers career progression assisted by Rear Admiral KASZ Raju another fine pilot who was the Assistant Chief of Personnel (Career Planning). Bhagwat claims that he was party to the contents. Pilots who serve together have a special bond and both Tahiliani and Raju flew the Sea Hawks on INS Vikrant with elan, and the subject was the talk of the Navy. Tahiliani had also secured an extension for Vice-Admiral J.G. Nadkarni so that he could succeed him, for which Nadkarni was grateful. Commodore Vishnu Bhagwat was Tahiliani's Naval Assistant and had been bloodied in the goings on in NHQ and the Defence Ministry at high levels. He had made good connections, which were to pay him dividends later to fight his case. The HDW scandal, Operation Brass Tacks, Sri Lanka foray 'Ops Pawan' and Bofors scandal had kept Rajiv Gandhi and the Defence Minister fully engrossed. Rajiv had left the daily running of the Defence Ministry to Arun Singh, the dapper Rhodes scholar, Minister of State for Defence who was very close to the Chiefs at that time - Tahiliani, Sundarji and La Fontaine. They held conclaves and seminars and there was much bon hommie. Arun Singh later abruptly resigned on the Bofors issue. The period had also seen a sudden expansion of the Naval Aviation Branch and as Navy Chief and Chairman Chiefs of Staff Committee Tahiliani an ace test pilot, felt obliged to support this Branch. It left a mark on the Navy, which is now struggling to get a replacement for INS Vikrant. So much for prospective planning of the times!

In personnel promotion matters, just before retiring, Tahiliani decided to combine two courses below the fourteenth NDA i.e. 15th and 16th for promotion to Rear Admiral and so the competition and vested interests at stake in the Board chaired by the outgoing Chief of Naval Staff in 1987 were larger, and his Writ ran. The fourteenth, fifteenth and sixteenth courses of the NDA were large courses and also comprised of a splendid spectrum of professionals which included Ravi Sharma, Bhandoola, N.S. Achreja, Peter Debrass the aviator, Kailash Kohli, Vijay Malhotra, Keki Pestonji, Avinish Tandon and Jagmohan Sodhi and Raja Menon, the last two submariners. Most officers considered at that board must have had excellent records and their career profiles spoke for themselves having served in latest front line ships, submarines and air squadrons. The Indian Navy had seen a spectacular and successful acquisition programme. Five Kashin Rajput class ships, aircraft carrier INS Viraat, three Godavari class Leanders, the Charlie class nuclear submarine Chakra, HDW and Kilo class submarines and Sea Harriers, Seaking MKBI and the 140 ton TU

142s ASW aircraft had joined the Fleet. Those were heady days for India's Cinderella service. The promotion board must have had a very difficult task and had to distribute officers branch-wise, as vacancies were limited to six for the prima donna executive branch. Bhagwat, Das, Kohli, Malhotra, Debrass, Tandon and Sodhi were cleared in the first board and Keki Pestonji and Raja Menon were promoted in their second look while P.D. Sharma, the pilot, in his third look. All was however not lost. Under a curious policy enunciated by Admiral R.H. Tahiliani the CNS and to ease matters, NHQ issued a policy directive that officers considered outstanding but not making it to Flag rank would be posted abroad as Naval or Defence Attaches. Navy also set in motion a policy to promote officers in second and third looks though most professional Navies decide either an officer at that level with some 26 years of service has Flag Officer qualities or not, if deep selection is resorted to. Navy also did not pursue a policy to assist bright officers not making the Flag Rank to go in for Public Sector posts. As per the new norms, I was posted out to Singapore in 1988 as Defence Advisor to Singapore, Phillipines and Thailand and was able to watch events in a detached manner and served to the best of my ability under some fine gentlemen Ambassadors of the Indian Foreign Service. I was also exposed to the free market economies, which was a rewarding experience.

So, this part of the story has to begin when in 1988, Bhagwat as Rear Admiral, after a brief spell in the DG DPS along with Major General Ashok Mehta. General Mehta a graduate of the Royal College of Defence Studies and Sri Lanka Op Pawan fame was obliged to resign along with four other Generals during the tenure of General Sunil Rodrigues, for allegedly not conforming to the standards of social etiquette expected of officers in the Army in dealing with brother officers wives. That controversial story was threaded in an issue of India Today. Mehta is now a journalist who has written extensively on Bhagwat in the Sunday magazine and claims he also has tendered a report on Bhagwat whilst the officer served in DGDPS. When I was leaving for Singapore, Bhagwat was appointed as the Chief of Staff to Flag Officer Commanding in Chief, Vice-Admiral S. Jain, at the HQWNC in Bombay and I recall wishing him well. It is a most coveted and professional appointment for a Rear Admiral and wields much responsibility and authority. It is true that since Bhagwat had had an excellent career profile, many felt he deserved it and the next step in normal circumstances, if all was equal, was that a Fleet Command would follow possibly the powerful Western Fleet.

Somehow Bhagwat got scents in 1989, that he was going to be by passed for command of the Fleet. Admiral J.G. Nadkarni the CNS was the training officer of the 15th course when they were midshipmen on INS Delhi. It is known that had a soft spot for that course. Bhagwat, thanks to his earlier appointments in NHQ had made good contacts. Well-wishers and informants in New Delhi seem to have kept him updated on the goings on in NHQ and the Defence Ministry. He seems to have consciously and systematically collected facts and data about all his immediate junior Rear Admirals to prove his case that all those below him suffered infirmities.

He kept tabs on many senior officers and his own Commanding-in-Chief's movements, ostensibly to ensure his security. He even made his way to personnel matters' file in HQWNC and retrieved the two separate covering letters forwarding his annual report of the period August 1988 to August 1989 written by Jain. This was something of a coup by Bhagwat and it is unusual to have two covering letters written 6 months apart for the report due around 1 Sep 1989. The first covering letter in original dated 13 September still lay in the file and Jain has always claimed even in an affidavit that such a report was only handed over seven months later on 26 March personally to the CNS and a covering Demi Official letter dated 28, March 1990 to NHQ substantiates this.

Bhagwat suspected foul play. Such things do happen in the rush and bustle of service life and cannot pass the test of legal questioning but can be judged as true or false, only by a test of what happens in service and the integrity of officers concerned. Bhagwat treasured the photocopies of both covering letters that stated his report of 1988–89 was forwarded to NHQ on different dates. On paper it seemed some error was afoot as there was only one report possible for the period. This doubt provoked Bhagwat, it appears, to feel that some skull duggery or plot was afoot and when he was not satisfied by interviews accorded by Jain, his immediate superior, and the CNS Nadkarni, he took this drastic action when he became aware that Kohli, his junior, was being appointed to the Western Fleet. The Navy issued a show cause notice to Bhagwat for having come into possession of personal and confidential correspondence from the confidential PA of Vice-Admiral Jain. Bhagwat, in his defence, stated that he had kept these two copies of covering letters as these pertained to proof of wrongdoing and was evidence of his case, so the laws of natural justice ruled in his favour and he was duty-bound to retain these in defence of his case as evidence. Legally it is said he had a point.

The Chief of Staff of a Command controls the Naval Analysis Unit (NAU), the counter intelligence wing of the Naval Intelligence akin to the Liasion Units of the Army and Air Force. These well trained plain clothes servicemen can ferret many a piece of information if asked to do so, and are supposed to report unusual activities and track targets' activities, mostly foreigners and suspected officers or men and those intimated by IB or RAW for surveillance. Bhagwat kept himself well informed of activities in the Command as a good Chief of Staff should and later used the knowledge in his representational Writ, it appears. Many were unaware that his wife, a brilliant lawyer, was penning these incidents and snippets down in legalese which finally surfaced as the massive Writ petition when Rear Admiral Kailash Kohli was secretly flown in from New Delhi by Nadkarni to take over the Western Fleet in Bombay from Rear Admiral I.S. Bedi of the 11th NDA course and also a graduate of Naval War College, USA, in an unprecedented mid-night take-over and early morning Divisions. The knife was brandished by Bhagwat's wife to Jain and filed in court in the form of a 404-page Writ. It shook the Cinderella service and caught many unawares. For the first time, many like me were educated by lawyer friends on the golf course and elsewhere what exactly a Writ meant, and how serious a matter it was. A Writ could redress wrongs. It could stay appointments. It could overturn decisions. It was serious business. Bhagwat and his lawyer wife sincerely believed Bhagwat was wronged. Some of the major elements highlighted in the Bhagwat's Writ were, much later, reproduced in a Public Interest Litigation No 1758 of 1996 filed by Shri Dilip Karambelkar in the Bombay High Court to stay Bhagwat's appointment as CNS. MoD has also bared clauses to defend the Defence Minister's actions. The whole makes interesting reading for analysis, and an extract from "My Presidential Years", by Shri R.V. Venkataraman is appended on the subject of Writs and PILs:

"The Chief Justice of India, Justice Pathak, and his wife came over one evening for tea. Justice Pathak is a serious, objective and mild-mannered gentleman who carries out his responsibilities with dignity. He candidly discussed many questions related to the judiciary such as the mounting arrears in court, the delay in appointment of judges and the expanding area of Writ jurisdiction. I pointed out that the liberal admission of Writ petitions, even when alternative remedies were available, was cluttering up the work of the higher judiciary. I also expressed my reservations about the liberal use of public interest litigation. Justice Pathak agreed with me that there was a need to be more selective about admissions and that he himself was not happy at the spate of public interest litigation."

HDW SUBMARINE DEAL AND OTHER ISSUES RAISED IN THE WRITS

The HDW is a deal that has dogged India. President Venkataraman, in his book, has revealed "Meanwhile, Rajiv Gandhi's problems began to intensify. The Indian Ambassador in Bonn sent a message saying that the German firm HDW, suppliers of SSK submarines, had quoted a higher price for two extra submarines as they claimed they had to pay a 7 per cent commission to "Indian contacts". Then, Swedish Radio, a private organisation, reported that the Swedish firm, Bofors, had paid commissions to Indian politicians and bureaucrats on the sale of 155mm Howitzer guns to India."

• Bhagwat took advantage of the HDW scam which had erupted and stated "From the years immediately prior to the period when the HDW Submarine contract/deal was negotiated there was a steady deterioration in the moral fabric of officers at the senior levels in the Indian Navy to the detriment of personnel policy, as highly placed Officers, succumbing to personal and pecuniary considerations."

• "Respondent No.2, Vice-Admiral Jain, while posted as Assistant Chief of Naval Staff (Policy and Plans) since 1st October 1980, was also involved in the negotiations of the SKS/HDW Submarine deal for extraneous considerations and the deal was signed on 1st December, 1981." "The said Respondent (S. Jain) was certifying availability of funds (free foreign exchange) and involved in behind the scenes negotiations "

• "Respondent No.4 (P.S. Das) was involved with the hurried negotiations to attempt to conclude a contract for the fifth and sixth Submarines HDW/SSK by 31 March 1986, presently under investigation."

• "Commodore P.S. Das continued to certify and confirm the availability of funds knowing fully well that this was not so, with consequential results of over expenditure of Rs.130 Crores for the financial years 1st April 1986 to 31 March 1987."

• "This matter was very serious. However, Respondent No.4 (P.S. Das) because of his relationship with Shri S.K. Bhatnagar, the then Defence Secretary was once again protected."

In the Writ Petition No.2757/90 Bhagwat complained that the key Naval appointments were being filled with Officers who had an USA linkage and more specifically alleged the following :-

☐ "In 198O, once again he (Vishnu Bhagwat) was first on the panel but Respondent No.4 (P.S. Das) was sent as he wanted to and he was Naval Assistant to the then Naval Chief, Admiral Periera, in whose tenure the HDW/SSK deal was first negotiated. It is not without significance that Respondent No.5 (K.K. Kohli) relieved Respondent No.4 (P.S. Das) as Naval Assistant to Admiral Periera. Further this reflects on the Service and has serious implications for security and intelligence.

☐ "It is not without coincidence that the chief of Naval Staff Admiral J.G. Nadkarni is ex-Naval War College, Newport, USA, the Respondent No.2 (S. Jain) is ex-Naval War College Newport, USA, the Flag Officer Commanding Western Fleet, Rear Admiral Bedi is ex-Naval War College Newport, USA, the appointment made to Eastern Fleet is of Rear Admiral P.S. Das (junior to Bhagwat), Ex-Naval War College Newport, USA, and the appointment announced of Rear Admiral K.K. Kohli who is also ex-Naval War College USA and junior to Petitioner."

.

☐ "All key appointments in the last few years were being held by Naval War College (New Port) USA alumni which on the face of it is a policy discriminatory to other outstanding officers (who have completed a higher defence course namely the National Defence College Course, New Delhi) and violative of Article 14 of the Constitution of India. This is not in the interest of National Security."

☐ "A 100% progression rate in the Navy to Flag Rank and Key Command position for Officers doing a course in any one foreign country as stated aforesaid is a matter of serious concern."

☐ "The World over experts on Military affairs acknowledge the key role that the US play upon structuring the policies of the Pakistan Government through the ISI and the Pakistan Army, this key factor is deliberately played down by most of the individuals who are US Naval War College alumni. Their progression in the Navy is supported in subtle (with few honourable exceptions)."

Bhagwat complained that then Honourable Prime Minister (Shri V.P.Singh) who was also holding the charge of Defence Ministry had failed in his duty as the Defence Minister. In a later case when the Appointments Committee of the Cabinet in 1998 took interest in Vice Admiral Harinder Singh's case and over ruled Bhagwat he stated the opposite that it was unimplimentible.

☐ The Defence Minister (Shri V.P.Singh) and the Appointment Committee of the Cabinet did not apply their mind to appointment/decision and were wholly influenced and guided by Respondent No.10 (Shri B.G. Deshmukh)."

☐ "There has therefore been absolute failure to protect National Security interests and vital changes have been effected in operational areas when such changes would have a serious negative effects for the "operations and the command chain" of the Navy."

☐ "The failure of the Defence Minister (Shri V.P. Singh) to grant a senior officer the Armed Forces a hearing as requested for in the statutory complaint to reveal sensitive matters relating to the appointments, arms deals, acquisitions and issues vital to National Security in spite of the of Punjab, Sri Lanka and Kashmir Valley is most unfortunate and regrettable."

☐ "As the Armed Forces represent the last bastion of Security for the Country and lowering of their morale, standards/fabric have grim repercussions for every nation in particular the developing countries. The statement that "corruption is akin to subversion applies more to the Armed Forces than to any other institution of the State,"

☐ "The Defence Ministry and the Defence Minister, who is also the Prime Minister (Shri V.P. Singh) and the Home Minister who is member of the Appointment Committee have failed to apply their minds to the fact that the Fleets now and hence Commands in future would have both inferior leadership (i.e. in fleet operations and tactics) and only morally pliable, morally culpable officers for whom self-interest would be predominant interest in violation of all principles Military Leadership would hold senior Command positions."

Bhagwat complained that Shri B.G. Deshmukh, the then Principal Secretary to the Prime Minister with his acts/omissions had created circumstances causing grave harm to the Naval as well as National Interests. Shri Deshmukh has written extensively in the media about this matter in his defence.

☐ "The Principal Secretary to the Prime Minister (Respondent No. 10) who is not the authority for recommending or scrutinising the proposal not being associated with the Ministry of Defence. He as Principal Secretary to the previous Prime Minister has regularly and illegally usurped the powers of the Defence Ministry, the Cabinet Secretary and the Joint Secretary in the Prime Minister's Secretariat dealing with Defence appointments and for reasons wholly extraneous to the appointments obtained the acquiescence of the Defence Minister (Shri V.P. Singh) who has not applied his mind to the serious implications of these proposals."

☐ "Respondent No.9 the then Defence Secretary in the Ministry of Defence who is aware of the activities of the Respondents 1, 2 and 3 (Nadkarni, Jain and Koppikar the Chief of Personnel). However, under the directions from the Minister of Defence (Shri V.P. Singh) under irregular advice of the Principal Secretary Mr. B.G. Deshmukh has acquiesced in the Order appointing Respondent No.5 (K.K. Kohli) Flag Officer Commanding Western Fleet in supercession of Petitioner therein."

☐ "In this case there has been a clear by-passing of procedure, criteria and norms for the appointment and only advice of Respondent No. 10 (B.G. Deshmukh) who in collusion with Respondent No.1 (J.G. Nadkarni) has prevailed and even the Cabinet Committee has not applied its mind and accepted the advice Principal Secretary to the Prime Minister."

Bhagwat contented that Admiral J.G. Nadkarni the then Chief of Naval Staff (Respondent No.4) with his acts/omissions had created circumstances causing grave harm with regard to Naval promotions/administration in the Navy and future growth of the Navy.

☐ "Respondent No.1 (J.G Nadkarni) utilised the services of Respondent No.10 (Shri B.G. Deshmukh), the Principal Secretary to the Prime Minister used an extra-Constitutional center of power not concerned with Defence appointments and having little knowledge the details of the files/proposals except the desire to influence decision making without any responsibility and to manipulate appointments with malafide intentions, when the Defence Minister Respondent No.11 (Shri V.P. Singh) who is also the Prime Minister as stated aforesaid was involved with disputes within his party and administratively too pre-occupied from applying his mind to a vital security appointment."

☐ "Respondent Nos.1, 2 and 3 (Nadkarni, Jain and Koppikar) with the assistance of Respondent No.10 (Shri B.G. Deshmukh) have been continuously misusing/utilising the intermittent periods of crisis from December, 1989 onwards facing the Government to push through illegal/irregular proposals and obtaining the Prime Minister's (Shri V.P. Singh) sanction when he has not been in a position as Defence Minister to apply his mind to the developments taking place in the Defence Ministry, being pre-occupied with other problems to the detriment of developments in Defence appointment vital to National Security."

☐ "Respondents Nos.1, 2 and 3 in collusion with a view to position and appoint Respondents No. 4, 5 and 6 (Das Kohli and Malhotra) and thereafter 6, 7 and 8 (Debrass and Tandon) as Fleet Commanders fabricated records in violation of Section 60 of the Navy Act to the detriment of National Security and indulged in acts of grave and serious consequences for the morale of the Indian Navy and of the Indian armed forces jeopardising National Security."

☐ "Further, Respondent No. 1 (J.G. Nadkarni) thought it necessary to position Respondent No. 3 (V.L. Koppikar) as Chief of Personnel to maintain confidentiality on the serious, illegal and irregular acts which have consistently taken place during his tenure as Chief of Naval Staff in close collusion with Respondent No.2."

☐ "The Respondent No.1 (J.G. Nadkarni), Respondent No.2 and 3 (Jain and Koppikar) and Respondent Nos. 4, 5 and 6 (Das Kohli and Malhotra) had a common objective to rid the Navy of those Officers who were inconvenient on account of their staunch nationalism moral integrity and strategic operational ability which they do not possess; as Respondents 1, 2 and 3 and Respondent Nos. 4, 5 and 6 are only committed to those Officers who serve their personal aims and objectives, and are ready to commit any act violative of all norms, rules and regulations, even prima facie illegal to secure their personal and immediate objective, the service comes only thereafter and the Country last of all in their objectives. All the above Respondents 1 to 6 have "a USA linkage in terms of war college course and/or children on scholarship receiving aid in USA and/or children with Green cards." The honest and professional officers in the Navy who have not attended War College (USA) do not desire these linkages and do not encourage their children to immigrate abroad/accept scholarships and/or aid from foreign Universities/Governments are subjected

to discrimination by Respondents 1, 2 and 3 herein.
Even honest Officers with children abroad are also
subjected to harassment."

☐ "The motivation as stated aforesaid of the
Respondent Nos. 1, 2 and 3 is to eliminate officers at
the level of Captains, Rear Admirals and above for
further progression who are not morally pliable and
who have the professionalism, the moral integrity and
determination to preserve the fighting spirit of the
Navy and the moral fire of its officers corps thereby
undermining the security of the country."

☐ "The distortion of Personnel Policies and
appointments and manipulations of confidential
reports primarily influenced by self-interest and for
personal/pecuniary considerations in the last nearly 3
years by Respondent No. 1 and 3 assisted wherever
concerned by Respondent No. 2 has lead to
widespread demoralisation in the Service."

☐ "These appointments of Fleet Commanders are
positively harmful to the Service and will destroy the
morale and professionalism of the Indian Navy which
has already received a grave setback from the facts
emerging from the HDW/SSK Submarine
investigation and other questionable arms/equipment
deals/contracts." .

☐ "The fact that the following Officers with
inferior records to the Petitioner have been sent as
Fleet Commanders was concealed from the Defence
Ministry and the Defence Minister (Shri V.P. Singh)
and Home Minister expected to protect the Security

interest of this country have not done so and allowed Respondent Nos. 1, 2 and 3 in collusion with Respondent No.10 (Shri B.G. Deshmukh) to deceive the Nation on Naval Leadership in spite of the fact that this Country is a Peninsula and the Lifeline of this Nation."

"In the said Writ Petition No.2757/90 the Bhagwat complained that Vice-Admiral Jain and the then Flag Officer commanding Western Naval Command, Bomba with his acts/omissions had caused grave harm with regard to naval promotion/administration in the Navy more specifically to him and alleged the following in the said Writ Petition :-

☐ "Respondents 1, 2 and 3 have prima facie colluded to replace and tamper with the Petitioner's report the late rendition of which is not covered by any rules and must be the subject matter of an administrative inquiry apart from the criminal liability involved for which the Petitioner is entitled to initiate separate proceedings."

☐ "The Respondent No.1 and 2 have acquired Flats in the Nau Sena Cooperative Housing Society, Versova, Bombay of which the actual construction cost is over Rs. 6,00,000/- and the cost of furnishing fittings etc. including marble fittings amounts to almost Rs. 2,00,000/-. This investment is beyond the means of the said Officers and the Respondents Nos. 1 and 2 have no other assets, shares, property, etc. as it is difficult for the officers to effect a net savings of Rs. 8 lakhs spent on the said Flat after maintaining the lavish standard of living which these Respondents are used to and fulfilling all family obligations. This has resulted in questionable appointments being made/proposed by Respondent No.1 and outstanding reports being given by Respondent Nos. 1 and 2 to morally pliable officers and sidelining of those like the Petitioner with moral and professional integrity."

In the said Writ Petition No.2757/90 Bhagwat also complained that Vice-Admiral P.S. Das's appointment as the Flag Officer commanding Eastern Fleet was malafide and had caused grave harm with regard to promotion in the Navy, more specifically the Respondent No.1 had inter alia, alleged the following :-

□ "The appointment of Respondent No.4 (P.S. Das) and Respondent No. 5 (K.K. Kohli) were clearly malafide in the view of the Petitioner's professional record, the flaws in the moral integrity of Respondent No.4, the linkages of Respondent No. 5."

□ "During the course of his professional career Respondent No. 4 (P.S. Das) was brought to Court Martial and convicted for fabricating documents for use in official proceedings during his Naval career and sentenced to six months loss of seniority."

□ "A ship of the Eastern Fleet INS Andaman sank during fleet exercises with loss of life, exposing the incompetence and negligence of Respondent No. 4 (P.S. Das)."

Bhagwat complained that Rear-Admiral K.K.

Kohli's (Respondent No.7) appointment as the then Flag Officer commanding Western Fleet had caused his supercession by Respondent No.1 and it had resulted in grave harm with regard to Naval promotions and progression in the Navy. These allegations are below :

☐ "Respondent No.5 (K.K. Kohli) had commanded inferior class of ships and belong to a family who went into the business of agency for Defence Equipment and Arms deals; black listing in respect of the said business took place way back in 1969 by Mr. H.C. Sarin, former Defence Secretary and the said firm was prohibited from access to the Defence Ministry and Army/Navy/Air Force Headquarters. The Respondent No.5, for favoured and ulterior considerations to Respondent No.1, is being positioned out of turn for the Fleet. The Respondent No.5 visited the USA last summer (1989) and paid a visit to the Naval War College, Newport (USA) without the permission of the Indian Mission."

Bhagwat complained against Rear Admiral V.K. Malhotra, the then Assistant Chief of Naval Operations, as below:

☐ "The Respondent No.6 (V.K. Malhotra) has commanded an inferior class of ships and was eased out of the Command peremptorily."

☐ "The Respondents Nos.5 and 6 (Jain and Malhotra) as is also well known in the services have been using vast fund at their disposal to subvert the integrity of Officers who are their superiors with a view to secure their immediate personal objectives."

Bhagwat complained against Rear Admiral A. Tandon, the then Assistant Chief of Naval Staff, as below:

☐ "The Respondent No.7 (Tandon) has brought in articles from aboard a ship without payment of customs duty which indicate the moral and professional integrity of the officers. These matters are on record in the Western Navy Command, yet no action has been taken by Respondents 1, 2 and 3, whereas the Petitioner has been subjected to grave harassment."

Similarly, Bhagwat had complained against Rear Admiral P. Debrass, the then Flag Officer, Goa Area, as below:

☐ "The Respondent No.8 (P. Debrass) has incurred a telephone bill of two and a half lakhs on private calls on a Government residential telephone which has not been paid till today. All the calls have been verified which the Officer eventually conceded though he first denied it."

Admiral J.G. Nadkarni the then chief of Naval Staff had brought out in his reply filed on 17 November, 1990 (in Writ Petition No.2757/90) the following points regarding competency as well as integrity of Bhagwat as reproduced below:-

☐ "This Honourable Court should not entertain this petition under Article 226 of the Constitution of

India as well appear from what is set out herein below, the Petitioner has made a number of false statements of facts, has misused improperly procured official record, has disclosed secret and confidential material in violation of the provisions of the Official Secrets Act and has consequently jeopardised the National Security. Furthermore the petition raises several disputed questions of facts."

☐ "Without prejudice to the aforesaid submissions, I respectfully submit that the Petition contains several wholly false scurrilous and irrelevant allegations and constitutes an abuse of the process of Court and should not therefore be entertained."

☐ "The 5th Respondent (K.K. Kohli) had an all-round record of service as well as of Sea Command in the rank of Captain as compared to the Petitioner (V. Bhagwat)."

☐ "The Petitioner had on occasions shown a discipline by passing superiors and failing to follow order which were not to his liking. He did so in 1983, when he was in the USSR as the head of Commissioning Crew of the INS Ranjit when he twice approached superior Soviet authorities without permission of the Naval Attache. The Petitioner received a very poor confidential report from his superior during this period."

☐ "When the Petitioner (V. Bhagwat) was in command of INS Ranjit from September, 1983 to December, 1985 out of sheer panic he almost opened fire on a Pakistani Maritime reconnaissance aircraft which came close to the ship. This panicky over-reaction was not a happy sign and showed a lack of fitness to hold the highly responsible post of Fleet Commander. It must we noted that any action by a Fleet Commander which is not a measured and rational action could have grave consequences."

☐ "Further when the Petitioner (Bhagwat) was commanding INS Ranjit there was an incident when one mid-shipman shot his own colleague and a sailor on duty by using a weapon belonging to the Ship which he had unauthorisedly drawn. Not only was the Petitioner as Commanding Officer responsible to ensure that weapons were kept in safe custody, when the matter was being investigated into by a Board of Enquiry, the petitioner declined to accept responsibility for lapses on his part but tried to pass on the blame to his subordinates. This was not considered a desirable quality and the petitioner was found culpable and was issued with a letter of displeasure for said lapses. I did not regard this as a desirable quality of a Fleet Commander."

☐ "Sometime in 1986, the Petitioner had suffered a heart attack and had been placed in the lower medical category S242 (Permanent) ever since because of his ischemic heart disease condition. The said category does not disentitle a person holding a Sea command but there are restrictions laid down. I, however, took this factor into consideration."

☐ "I had personally noticed that the Petitioner tended to be extremely tense and was unable to relax. This resulted in a domestic tragedy in as much as his son ran away from home. I did not regard these traits as sound psychological traits in a person who would be holding a very sensitive command, requiring in emergency conditions, to take instant decisions likely to have grave repercussions."

☐ "Further in October, 1989 I had asked the opinion of three Flag Officers Commanding-in-Chief of the commands who in their opinion was the best person to command the Western Fleet, when a vacancy was likely to arise in 1990. None of the three Flag Officers mentioned the name of the Petitioner as a person recommended by them. The said decision, as mentioned herein above, was taken by me independently on consideration of relevant factors and it is incorrect to allege that there was any impropriety whatever in providing the suggesting the appointment of the 5th Respondent (K.K Kohli) to the said post or that the 2nd Respondent (S. Jain) had anything whatsoever to do with the said decision which was duly approved by the Appointments Committee of the Cabinet."

Vice-Admiral S. Jain, the then Flag Officer Commanding-in-Chief Western Naval Command, Bombay, (Respondent No.5 herein) had also filed on 17 November, 1990, an affidavit in reply (in Writ Petition No.2757/90) countering each and every allegations, contentions and submissions of Vishnu Bhagwat regarding the character and integrity of Bhagwat as reproduced below:-

☐ "I had told the Petitioner (V. Bhagwat) that I had given him a good confidential report which, however, had only been forwarded in March, 1990. The Petitioner at the same time was informed by me about weaknesses in his character which were reflected in his confidential report. It is correct that I told the Petitioner that if he so desired, he could meet the Chief of Naval Staff in April, 1990 during the latter's visit to Bombay."

☐ "The original covering letter dated 13th September, 1989 was returned by me to my SPA Mrs. Dsouza who thereafter kept it in the confidential file relating to confidential report on officers of Flag Rank i.e. same as the Petitioner. The Petitioner (V. Bhagwat) unauthorisedly got hold of the said file during my absence from Station and xeroxed the said original letter dated 10th September, 1989 and the Office copy of the ditto letter dated 28 March, 1990 and forwarded xerox copies of the same to the Minister of Defence and others. The very fact that the original letter bearing the crest of the command and signature remained in the file conclusively proves that I had never submitted any report in September, 1989." Moreover the letter dated 28 March 1990 clearly shows that the delay in submitting the confidential reports related not only to the Petitioner but also to other officers, namely Vice-Admiral (then Rear admiral) KASZ Raju and Rear Admiral J.J. Baxi. There was also a delay in submitting the confidential reports of some other officers, namely Commodore H. Sahney, Commodore R. Shah, Commodore R.R. Navi and Captain A. Barla and Commander A.R. Radhakrishnan."

The facts and circumstances in which the said

Writ Petition No.2757/90, was filed and the repercussions of such Writ Petition at that point of time were extensively covered by the Press. These pointers are highlighted for the reader.

☐ "The Petition was filed at a significant moment. It was filed first a fortnight before the announcement of the next chief was to be made." (India Today, October 1990)

☐ "Nadkarni is due to retire on November 30, and the main contenders for the top job are Jain and his counterpart from the Eastern Naval Command Vice-Admiral L. Ramdas, whom Bhagwat is personally very close to." (India Today, October 1990).

☐ "Sharp differences had already emerged between Jain and Bhagwat over day to day functioning of the command. The tension was further accentuated by Bhagwat's pro-Soviet ideology and his belief that Jain along with Nadkarni and Kohli, all of whom having done a course at Naval War College, Newport, were part of a pro-US coterie dominating the Navy." (India Today, dated October 1990, page55).

☐ "But things changed dramatically with Rear Admiral Bhagwat's Writ Petition. Though the Petition was filed in protest against his candidature for the Fleet Admiral's post being overlooked in favour of Rear Admiral K.K. Kohli, the 400-page document really in the nature of allegations of a very personal nature against top Naval officers and their alleged links with foreign powers." (Sunday Observer, 21

October, 1990).

☐ "The wide scope of Bhagwat's Petition has therefore invited the charge that it is also these factors." (India Today, October 1990).

☐ "While Bhagwat's petition is inspired by his non-appointment, its content and more significantly some crucial omissions, have raised a doubt whether it has also been provoked by the desire to strengthen Ramdas's candidature over Jain for the post of Naval Chief." (India Today October 1990).

☐ "It was pointed out that the children of Jain as well as other sons of top officers were settled in the US. Strangely, the petition did not mention the instance of Vice-Admiral Ramdas whose three daughters are green-card holders." (Sunday Observer, dated 21 October, 1990). "One of them, Kavita, is also married to a Pakistani, Zulfiqar Ahmed, who is specialising in comparative studies of the Soviet Union (when contacted by India Today, Ramdas declined to say anything about the controversy)." (India Today, October 1990).

☐ "Similarly, Bhagwat reserves his most vitriolic attack for Rear Admiral P.S. Das, who was appointed to command the Eastern Fleet. He holds him personally responsible for the sinking of the INS Andaman on August, 21 and repeatedly draws attention to this fact. However, there is no mention at all of the FOC-IN-C East, Vice-Admiral L. Ramdas, who was also present at sea during the exercises in which INS Andaman sank and had overall responsibilities of the Fleet." (India Today, October, 1990).

☐ "The Bhagwat Petition filed by his advocate-wife, Niloufer Bhagwat, also raised questions about a number of defence deals. The wrong-doings, it would appear, were known to Bhagwat for many years, but he has raised them now and thus, cast aspersions on several top officers, both senior and junior to him...." "Navy sources point out that several of these deals were approved when President R. Venkatraman, either the Defence Minister or the Finance Minister. "Is Ramdas suggesting an investigation against the President?" asked an officer who claimed that the petition was entirely motivated." (Sunday Observer, dated 21 October, 1990).

☐ "According to top Naval and defence sources Ramdas began to lobby to strengthen his case against Jain. He made three personal trips to the Capital and according to Naval officials, began lobbying with bureaucrats in Defence Ministry and the newly-appointed Minister of State for Defence, Dr. Raja Ramanna." (India Today, October 1990).

☐ "One of the Ramdas daughters, Kavita to a Pakistan National Zulfiqar Ahmed..." The Ramdas family flew to the US to attend the marriage on April 28, significantly, he did not report this alliance - as is customary in the Armed Forces - prior to him being announced as the chief of Naval Staff designate." (Sunday Observer, 21 October, 1990).

☐ "The Respondent said that Ramdas took the

permission of the then Union Minister of State for Defence, Raja Ramanna to attend his daughters marriage on April 28, 1990, in the USA. (Free Press Journal, 30 November 1990).

☐ "The drowning of "INS Andaman" which developed engine trouble on August 21, during an exercise in the Bay of Bengal, raises similar excitement in Navy circles. The exercise was being conducted by Vice-Admiral Ramdas. It is said that sinking of a warship in peacetime is an unprecedented event and suggesting either gross neglect of ship's maintenance or neglect of duty or both. An enquiry into the episode has been set up. But Navy services are sceptical about whether it will get to the truth. This is because pressure is believed to have been brought to bear on the highest quarters, to have a board of a board of enquiry to be headed by a Rear Admiral. Firstly, this is a departure from the usual practice of entrusting such enquiries to a Naval Captain. Secondly, the Rear admiral heading the enquiry happens to be the chief of staff to Vice-Admiral Ramdas." (Sunday Observer, 21 October, 1990).

☐ "The following day, August 21, while the Andaman was desperately fighting for survival, Ramdas left taking Das with him, leaving behind the Andaman and two other ships, whose Commanding Officers were junior to the Commanding Officer of the Andaman." (Blitz dated 27 October 1990).

Shri Dilip Karambelkar had this to represent in the PIL he filed. "It is interesting to note that Bhagwat had made serious allegations against top Senior officers of the Indian Navy and also the top bureaucracy of the Central Government and therefore, to allow the withdrawal of the said Writ Petition without examining and ascertaining veracity, or otherwise, of the serious complaints and allegations made by Respondent No.1 herein (Petitioner therein), had left in the public mind serious questions regarding the safety, security and integrity of the Nation and also regarding the method and manner in which the Ministry of Defence in particular, and the Govt of India in general has been functioning. Hence the need for this Writ Petition."

"It is already public knowledge that since the Honourable Supreme Court had systematically passed orders in respect of Hawala case, Urea case, Jharkhand Mukti Morcha case, Housing scandal and Lakhubhai Pathak's case to allow in-depth examination by the Central Bureau of Investigation and such other investigations, and to allow the law of the land to prevail equally over the people in power, political leaders and others, therefore, the Petitioner herein humbly submits that in the interest of justice and public interest and in the interest of safety, security and integrity of the Nation, the allegations made by Bhagwat (Respondent No.1 herein Petitioner therein) in the said Writ Petition No.2757/90 as well as the affidavits in reply, both dated 17-11-90, containing serious counter allegations filed by Vice Admiral Jain (Respondent No.4 herein Respondent No.1 therein) and Vice Admiral Koppikar (Respondent No.5 herein Respondent No.2 therein) do require in-depth and thorough judicial examination by this Honourable court."

"The allegations made by Respondent No.1 (Bhagwat) in the said Writ Petition No.2757/90 are so wild on a first look at them that, subsequent withdrawal of the said Writ Petition shows that Bhagwat has utilised the Writ Petition to boost his own personal career in the Navy by throwing muck at senior/superior officers not only in the Navy but in the Central Government as well. The manner in which the said Writ Petition No.2757/90 was withdrawn after the Bhagwat found conducive atmosphere with the elevation of Respondent No.3 (Ramdas) herein to the post of the Chief of Naval Staff, shows that the said Writ Petition was, for all practical purposes, a blackmail of the decision-making quarters in the Navy, in the Ministry of Defence and also the Senior Secretaries of Union of India. Since, the Respondent No.1 (Bhagwat) is also a candidate now being considered for the post of the Chief of Naval Staff, it will be in national interest as well as in the interest of justice, to examine the conduct of Respondent No.l in filing and withdrawing the said Writ Petition No.2757 of 1990."

"That the three candidates who are now being considered for the post of Chief of Naval Staff i.e. Vishnu Bhagwat, P.S. Das and K.K. Kohli, are the Officers against whom thick cloud of suspicion regarding their integrity and competence were raised in one form or the other either through the said Writ Petition or through the counter affidavits filed by S. Jain and V.K. Koppikar (Respondent No.1 and 2 therein) before this Honourable court. Therefore, it is in the National interest and in the interest of justice that, these thick clouds of suspicion are thoroughly and properly examined to find out the veracity falsity of the allegations/counter allegations, all made in the name of national safety, security and integrity."

"That the issue of HDW/SSK submarine deal and the possible alleged kickbacks thereof, which show that HDW/SSK issue is similar to the issues of Hawala case, Urea case, Lakhubhai Pathak cheating case, Jharkhand Mukti Morcha pay-off case, Central Government Housing scandal and other scandals being examined by the Honourable Supreme Court and High Courts of the Country."

Conclusion

After completing the research into this Mahabharat that took place and exposing all the fussilades launched by Bhagwat and another interested party in the Bombay High court to oppose his appointment as CNS, (which documents today form public records,) I want to make it clear that I have written the aforesaid as a duty to my country-men and the history of the Indian Navy that gave me succour for thirty two years. I leave it to readers and analysts to make their own judgements of the case of Vishnu Bhagwat as its reverberations finally made history and the BJP government fell on 17, April 1999 as its side effect. The Ministry of Defence issued a 124-page booklet in April 1999 on the subject of Vishnu Bhagwat without any heading or any acknowledgement. It rambles on from event to event without conjunction and confuses the reader because it also includes all the copious correspondence between the Ex-Prime Minister H.D. Deve Gowda and the Minister of Defence on the case of the T-72 tanks which Gowda recommends and the choice of the Government of the T 80s. Some extracts from that document are reproduced below.

(A) A paragraph on the report rendered by his immediate superior Vice Admiral S. Jain, FOC-in-C Western Command, had this to say about Rear Admiral Vishnu Bhagwat:

"Bhagwat has made viciously malicious and false accusations.... is a disgruntled officer who is also mentally unbalanced. He is schizophrenic and needs psychiatric help.... has developed a sinister information-gathering network within the service and the Government for ulterior motives.... has been spying on his superiors, subordinates and peers.... has not hesitated to tap telephones.... has rifled through desk of others".

(B) Another statement of the Government:

"How can any Government have confidence in the motives and integrity of the officer like Admiral Vishnu Bhagwat who in his own testimony, had affirmed that it is the Defence Minister who must sit in judgement over the proposals of the Chief of Naval Staff or else the morale of the Service will be destroyed but when this very question was posed to him, as Chief of Naval Staff, and was asked to reconsider a certain proposal of his, lest it leads to loss of morale in the Service, he denied the Raksha Mantri any jurisdiction or knowledge on morale in the

Navy."

(C) The MOD booklet also clearly indicates that Admiral Vishnu Bhagwat used the technique of levelling charges with part truths and has this to say:

"Given such a background, the allegations levelled by the ex-Chief of Naval Staff deserve to be treated with utter contempt. In view, however, of the persistent and motivated campaign which has been unleashed by interested quarters citing these very allegations, it has become necessary to set the records straight."

(D) Another paragraph goes, thus:

"The ex-Chief of Naval Staff did not stop at lying. When Vice Admiral Sushil Kumar finally felt compelled to write to the Government (to which he was legally entitled) for redressal of his statutory complaint which had been kept pending by the Chief of Naval Staff (the Naval Regulations provide for time-bound disposal of such representations), on 24th November 1998, the Chief of Naval Staff threatened him over on the telephone on 27th November 1998. A detailed account of the events is given in the booklet.

All this makes for hapless reading and future generations of the Navy should ensure a Bhagwat does not reoccur in the high offices of the Chief of Naval Staff as much trust is enjoined in that office to defend the motherland and treat each and every officer and sailor with the respect he or she duly deserves . Amen

SWORDS WERE OUT AGAINST BHAGWAT MUCH EARLIER

Britain's Royal Navy was notorious for its harsh discipline and for good reason. Since a good many sailors in the 17th and 18th centuries were pressed into service many unwillingly to serve under professional Masters and Captains, and many sailors on board were convicts asked to serve reduced sentences at sea so a firm hand was often needed to keep the crews in line. All of the Royal Navy's punishments were listed in a document entitled. 'The Articles of War, which were originally drawn up in the 1660s and later to become the Royal Navy Discipline Act which Indian Navy adopted with few changes only and it had Courts Martial rules different from the Army and Air Force.

The modus operandi how Admiral Vishnu Bhagwat was removed from his post as the Chief of Naval Staff (CNS) by the left over British legacy of 'Presidential Pleasure' was enacted in to India's Constitution on 29th November, 1949 and how knives were out for him even earlier to deny him a Fleet Command as Rear Admiral and was superseded by his two juniors, the communications specialist Rear Admirals PS Das and navigator Kailash Kohli by the Joint Secretary (Navy) reportedly Bambit Roy who had dealt with Bhagwat earlier and the Chief of

Naval Staff Admiral JG Nadkarni. It needs noting Nadkarni, Das and Kohli were graduates of the Naval War College Rhode Island USA which has an unwritten code like Harvard and US colleges have , to help each other to grow, Bhagwat was not from NWC.

Bhagwat had penned derogatory remarks in his Writ Petition to claim the Fleet commander appointment that there was a click of US trained and naval officers with children in USA for studies or working. Both Vishnu and his wife Nilopher had spent over a year in the Soviet Union standing by the powerful INS Ranjit which he commanded and his views about USA were coloured.

It is well known that US Navy F-4 Tomcat supersonic planes can fly low and slow with flaps down and an F-4 trailed INS Ranjit when Bhagwat was in command and over flew the ship many times possibly taking pictures. Capt Vishnu Bhagwat switched on Ranjit's Volna anti-aircraft system the naval equivalent of the Air Forces Pechora, and locked on to the F-4 and though it scooted away the US Embassy took it up with MOD and may be the JS (N) had to tender apologies as locking on to a known friendly force with weapon systems in peace time, is not done. Also Bhagwat had an unfortunate gun firing incident on board that led to a death. All these mattered and were brought up later.

This is a back ground but facts have now come to light that when Admiral RH Tahiliani also a graduate of NWC USA was the Chief of Naval Staff (CNS) in 1985-86 he found the Navy had become truly three dimensional with over 18 submarines and INS Chakra was to arrive as he retired. Navy's aircraft strength had swiftly gone up with Dornier-228s, 30 Sea Harriers, Kirans, IL-38s and TU-142s. He had to do balancing and bring up the aviators and others.

Cmde Vishnu Bhagwat was appointed to the key post of Naval Assistant to CNS in NHQ as a Commodore and a promotion board was due for Commodores/Captains to Rear Admiral. Vacancies were few and CNS realised that if only two courses 13th and 14th of the NDA were taken up there were too many surface Captains who had qualifying outstanding Annual Confidential Reports (ACRS) like Ranjit Rai who had also faced a navigational court martial and acquitted, Premvir Das who had faced a courts martial as a Lt on INS Cannnore with loss of seniority, Ravi Sharma, Suresh Bhandoola and George Kailath left over from earlier batches who were allowed three chances would take up all vacancies and leave a drought for submarine and aviation officers in later courses.

In fairness to CNS late Admiral Tahiliani he expanded the batch from 13th up to 16th course to accommodate others. Bhagwat and Premvir Das a very bright officer nephew of Ambassador Naresh Chandra and his brother RAW Chief Gary Saxena of the 14th course both commissioned on 1st Jan, 1960 and the six months junior Kailash Kohli another bright officer were promoted on the same day in that seniority. A letter stating outstanding officers who had missed Flag Rank would be sent abroad to missions as attaches.

George Kailath was sent to London, Ranjit Rai was sent to Singapore, Bhandoola to Washington DC and Ravi Sharma who was Navigating officer on INS Betwa when Cdr Tahiliani was the Captain had earlier been sent to Singapore. The letter was soon cancelled.

Cmde Vishnu Bhagwat as NA had helped CNS Tahiliani to make a chart of all Admirals progression and Bhagwat was slated to become Chief of Staff Western Naval Command (WNC) as Rear Admiral and then to command the Western Fleet as FOCWF. Bhagwat did become Chief of Staff Mumbai and was sure of Western Fleet Command. Rear Admiral Premvir Das his junior took over the Eastern Fleet, but doubts arose when Vice Admiral JG Nadkarni did not retire as due. Tahiliani had arranged that Nadkarni who had served with him and had defended him in a navigational courts martial when Tahiliani was the Captain of Vikrant was to tipped to become the first Chairman of the Jawahar Nehru Port Trust (JNPT). Tahiliani was acquitted in the courts martial.

Nadkarni became the Vice Chief of Naval Staff (VCNS) and . Vice Admiral S Jain also graduate of NWC USA the FOC-in-C was being considered for the CNS post as next senior most as Nadkarni would have retired.

A new turn of events took place in 1985. Prime Minister Rajiv Gandhi asked RK Malhotra Indian Administrative Service (IAS) former Secretary Finance, who was India's Executive Director of the International Monetary Fund (IMF) in USA to return and take over the appointment as Governor of the RBI, as it was vacant. His wife Anna Ranjan Malhotra was the first woman member of the.IAS and he agreed if Anna got a job in Mumbai. PMO and Appoinments committee agreed to make Anna the Chairman of JNPT. Later CNS Tahiliani got Nadkarni an extension and Admiral Jayant G Nadkarni Became CNS on '1st December, 1987 and

in his time Kailash Kohli flew down to Mumbai
without Bhagwat the Chief of Staff's knowledge to
take over the Western Fleet at night from Rear
Admiral IK Bedi. Bhagwat's wife tabled a writ
petition in the Mumbai High Court and a statutory
complaint after his first complaint three months
earlier, both landed up on Additional Secretary MOD
NN Vohra's table under the Navy Act which reads.

Section 23 in The Navy Act, 1957
23. Remedy of aggrieved persons.—
(1) If an officer or sailor thinks that he has
suffered any personal, oppression, injustice or other
ill-treatment at the hands of any superior officer, he
may make a complaint in accordance with the
regulations made under this Act.
(2) The regulations referred to in sub-section (1)
shall provide for the complaint to be forwarded to the
Central Government for its consideration if the
complainant is not satisfied with the decision on his
complaint.

A note from the Additional secretary brought out,
informs CNS Jayant Nadkarni a very sharp mind that
Bhagwat's writ and statutory are with MOD for reply
and asks how as senior most Rear Admiral Bhagwat
was denied Fleet Command. CNS explained that a
matrix was made out and in that matrix, Kohli came
on top, Das came second and Bhagwat third and as
there were only two fleets they were appointed
accordingly and added it was the prerogative of CNS
to appoint Fleet Commanders. JS Navy had approved
the matrix additional secretary was told.
The Additional Secretary MOD asked CNS why

the Army 'modus operandi' to give Divisional Commands by seniority could not be followed by the Navy and asked date a Fleet post would fall vacant and CNS indicated it would be Eastern Fleet when Das would complete one year. MOD and Appointments Committee approved Bhagwat's name for the Eastern Fleet and there was relief when he withdrew the writ. The swords were out from and Bhagwat became a Vice Admiral and by seniority became CNS on 1st October, 1996 and on 30th December, 1998 CNS Admiral Vishnu Bhagwat was removed from his post before he could take over as Chairman Chiefs of Staff Committee which modus operandi is again briefly explained.

Re-explaining the use of 'Presidential Pleasure' to get it amended

'Presidential Pleasure' has actually become a handle for Chiefs and Government to waive before an officer as a threat to offer resignation (War room leak in point) and if he does not relent, then dismiss him even on flimsy grounds under 'Presidential Pleasure' with no re-course to appeal or legal locus to approach Courts. This law was legislated by Britain as the British military was deployed world over in colonies and it was done so that any British Defence Service Officer or Sailor, Soldier and Airman could be removed in a foreign land by the senior most Crown representative in National Interests of the Crown and be repatriated to Britain for an inquiry/ trial. This was entered in to the Indian Constitution though UK has no written Constitution in Articles 310/311 despite Justice Shah a legal luminary explaining to Pandit Nehru that an officer in India could be suspended and inquired as India was a composite state but Nehru did not heed it. Justice Shah then suggested then the art 310 be added with a clause that the President would be obliged 'to apply his mind' and Nehru retorted the President shall have no powers as India is not a Presidential system. Hence the methodology of employing Presidential Pleasure for dismissal is more or less left to the Defence Minister to keep few informed.

In 1957 Indian Navy adopted the Royal Navy Discipline Act as Indian Navy Act 1957 and so the fire brand Defence Minister George Fernandes in the BJP Government could employ Art 310 entered in to the Navy Act 1957 as Section 15 (i) which reads, " Every officer and sailor shall hold office during the Pleasure of the President.

Fernandes was in a powerful position and with NSA Brijesh Misra who had confidence of PM Atal Behari Vajpayee could flag national interests as raison de'etre to act and flew in Bhagwat's relief Vice Admiral Sushil Kumar from his command in Cochin secretly in a Research & Analysis wing (RAW) and unceremoniously withdraw trust of the "Presidential Pleasure", Ministry of Defence Vide Letter 6301/AS(D) 98 dated 30th December, 1998 Vide Letter.

The Ministry of Defence led a sustained campaign of attrition against Admiral Vishnu Bhagwat, but the specific charges against him have been found to be of dubious value when examined against documentary record. Sukumar Muralidharan writing in Frontline states Fernandes alleged that Admiral Bhagwat had endangered national security through some of his actions, but that he was not at liberty to reveal these for reasons which should be self-evident (Frontline, January 29, 1999).

On 7th March, Sukumar wrote that in the case of Admiral Vishnu Bhagwat, former Chief of the Naval Staff, has been contested through a sustained campaign of attrition in the media. Specific charges against the Admiral were found to be of dubious value when examined against the documentary record. And as his ramparts crumbled in the battle against the recalcitrant military commander, Defence Minister George Fernandes sought recourse to the enigmatic slogan of national security. Fernandes alleged that Admiral Bhagwat had endangered national security through some of his actions, but that he was not at liberty to reveal these for reasons which should be self-evident.

The article for an aggrieved officer or sailor to appeal any personal, oppression, injustice or other ill-treatment is given in the Navy Act below and that is the route Rear Admiral Vishnu Bhagwat took in the 1980s when he was denied the command of the Fleet and superseded by two of his juniors and had gone to the Mumbai High Court represented by Mrs Nilopher a senior lawyer at the bar. Also Admiral Bhagwat could not be Courts Martialed as the President of the five member board would have to be senior to Bhagwat as per Navy Act 1957. The only person who was senior to Bhagwat was the President as the Supreme Commander in the Constitution so removing Bhagwat under President's Pleasure was the only safe option. .

TERMS

CNO: Chief of Naval Operations
ACNS: Assistant Chief of Naval Staff
CNS: Chief of Naval Staff
DCNS: Deputy Chief of Naval Staff
FOC-in-C : Flag Officer Commanding-in-Chief
GoC-in-C: General Officer Commanding-in-Chief
INS: Indian Naval Ship
MoD: Ministry of Defence
PIL: Public Interest litigation
RADM: Rear Admiral
RM: Raksha Mantri (Defence Minister)
NDA: National Defence Academy
NHQ: Naval Head Quarters
Shri: word akin to Mr.
Shrimati: Word Akin to Mrs.
USI: The United Service Institution of India
VCNS: Vice Chief of Naval Staff

ABOUT THE AUTHOR

Commodore (Retired) Ranjit B. Rai joined the NDA as a term mate of Admiral Vishnu Bhagwat in 1955 as part of the 14th course. Rai has served in appointments similar to Bhagwat as Flag Lt, Commanded Fleet Ships as a Commander and Captain and held the post of Fleet Operations Officer in Western Fleet. He served as Director of Naval Intelligence in NHQ at the same time that Bhagwat was Naval Assistance to the Chief of Naval Staff. The close association continued and Ranjit Rai retired in 1993 to pursue a career in International Shipping. He enjoys writing and commentates on Defence Affairs. He is author of – A Nation and Its Navy at War(Lancers), Indians Why we are What we are (Manas) and Golf ,The Inner Mental Game. He is a graduate of RN Staff College Greenwich London and has served four years in S.E.Asia as Defence Adviser from 1988-1992. As a love of labour to record the historical sacking of the Chief of Naval Staff and events thereafter he undertook to write this book to educate, enlighten and sift fact from fiction in a readable manner. His interests are golf and writing.

Get Published with Frontier India

Getting your work published is a wish for many for reasons including profit earning, self-satisfaction, popularity and other good reasons. You might even want to republish your book which is currently out of print.. Frontier India Technology as a publisher, distributor and retailer of books, offers a complete range of publishing, editorial, and marketing services that helps you as an author to take his or her book to the reader. We will offer you choices based on your needs. Get in touch with us at frontierindia@gmail.com.

Our Recently Published Military Books include :

An Indian Air force Recollects by Wing Co P.K. Karayi (Retd.) ISBN: 978-8193005507

Warring Navies – India and Pakistan (International Edition) – by Cmde Ranjit B. Rai (Retd.). Joseph P. Chacko. ISBN: 978-8193005545

Foxtrot to Arihant – The Story of Indian Navy's Submarine Arm by Joseph P. Chacko. ISBN: 978-8193005552

Foxtrots of the Indian Navy by Cmde P.R Franklin. ISBN: 978-8193005576

A Nation and its Navy at War by Cmde Ranjit Rai. ISBN: 978-8193005583

Handbook of Submarine Operations Cmde P.R Franklin. ISBN: 978-8193005590/ 978-9385699016